Poverty Reduction, Education, and the Global Diffusion of Conditional Cash Transfers

Michelle Morais de Sá e Silva

Poverty Reduction, Education, and the Global Diffusion of Conditional Cash Transfers

palgrave
macmillan

Michelle Morais de Sá e Silva
Escola Nacional de Administração
   Pública (ENAP)
Brasília, Brazil

ISBN 978-3-319-85060-3   ISBN 978-3-319-53094-9   (eBook)
DOI 10.1007/978-3-319-53094-9

Cover illustration: © Astrakan Images/Alamy Stock Photo

Printed on acid-free paper

This Palgrave Macmillan imprint is published by Springer Nature
The registered company is Springer International Publishing AG
The registered company address is: Gewerbestrasse 11, 6330 Cham, Switzerland

To my children João Pedro and Manuela, my greatest sources of motivation and strength.
To my love Fabio, my partner in the adventures of life.

Acknowledgements

As this has been a multiyear project, it is almost impossible to be comprehensive in thanking everyone who has played a role in it. So in general terms, I would like to thank all of those who agreed to be interviewed for the research that gave life to this book, ranging from teachers and school principals to ministers and senators. I should also thank Fulbright and Brazil's Coordination for the Improvement of Higher Education Personnel, whose funds were essential for the development of this project.

Particularly, I must thank two great women scholars who have provided guidance and motivation for my scholarly work. I thank Prof. Gita Steiner-Khamsi, who has been a great mentor, even beyond my Ph.D. years at Teachers College, Columbia University. I should also thank Prof. Kathryn Sikkink, who encouraged me to put together the book proposal during my fellowship at the Carr Center for Human Rights Policy at the Harvard Kennedy School of Government. Both of them are excellent and generous professors who have been an inspiration to generations of young scholars.

I should also thank Kenia Ketley, a dedicated research assistant who allowed me to go through the nuts and bolts of finalizing the manuscript. At Palgrave Macmillan, various editorial contacts supported this project throughout its different phases and Milana Vernikova was the one who helped me get it done, always very thoughtful and caring. I thank her for all her support and patience.

Finally, I should thank my family and my team at Brazil's National School of Public Administration, who bore with me throughout the year of manuscript writing and whose support was absolutely essential for this book to come to life.

CONTENTS

ABBREVIATIONS

ABC   *Agência Brasileira de Cooperação* (Brazilian Cooperation Agency)
AIG   American International Group
CAB   Citizens Advice Bureau
CCT   Conditional Cash Transfer
CEO   Center for Economic Opportunity, Mayor's Office
CIDER   *Centro Interdisciplinario de Estudios sobre Desarrollo*
            (Development Studies Interdisciplinary Center)
DFID   Department for International Development
DOE   Department of Education
EdLabs   Education Innovation Laboratory
EFA   Education for All
Enade   *Exame Nacional de Desempenho de Estudantes* (National
            Assessment of Student Performance)
Enem   *Exame Nacional do Ensino Médio* (National High School Exam)
Fedesarrollo *Fundación para la Educación Superior y el Desarrollo* (Foundation
            for Higher Education and Development)
FSSAP   Female Secondary School Assistance Program (Bangladesh)
FODESEP   *Fondo de Desarrollo de la Educación Superior* (Higher Education
            Development Fund)
Fundeb   *Fundo de Manutenção e Desenvolvimento da Educação Básica
            e de Valorização dos Profissionais da Educação* (Fund for the
            Maintenance and Development of Basic Education and the
            Valorization of Education Professionals)
GDP   Gross Domestic Product

HDI   Human Development Index
IBGE   *Instituto Brasileiro de Geografia e Estatística* (Brazilian Institute of Geography and Statistics)
IDB   Inter-American Development Bank
Ideb   *Índice de Desenvolvimento da Educação Básica* (Index of Basic Education Development)
IGD   *Índice de Gestão Descentralizada* (Index of Decentralized Management)
ILO   International Labor Organization
IMF   International Monetary Fund
IPC-IG   International Policy Center for Inclusive Growth
IPEA   *Instituto de Pesquisas Econômicas Aplicadas* (Institute of Applied Economic Research)
LDB   *Lei de Diretrizes e Bases da Educação Nacional* (National Educational Bases and Guidelines Law)
MDGs   Millennium Development Goals
MDRC   Manpower Demonstration Research Corporation
MDS   *Ministério do Desenvolvimento Social e Combate à Fome* (Ministry of Social Development and Fight Against Hunger)
MDSA   *Ministério do Desenvolvimento Social e Agrário* (Ministry of Social and Agrarian Development)
MESA   *Ministério Extraordinário de Segurança Alimentar e Combate à Fome* (Especial Ministry of Food Security and Fight Against Hunger)
MIT   Massachusetts Institute of Technology
MoE   Ministry of Education
NIS   *Número de Identificação Social* (Number of Social Identification)
NPO   Neighborhood Partner Organization
NYC   New York City
OSI   Open Society Institute
PSAT   Preliminary Scholastic Assessment Test
PDT   *Partido Democrático Trabalhista* (Democratic Labor Party)
PNAD   *Pesquisa Nacional por Amostra de Domicílios* (National Household Survey)
PPP   Purchasing Power Parity
PRS   Poverty Reduction Strategy
PRSPs   Poverty Reduction Strategy Papers
PSDB   *Partido da Social Democracia Brasileira* (Brazilian Social Democratic Party)
PT   *Partido dos Trabalhadores* (Workers' Party)

SECADI   *Secretaria de Educação Continuada, Alfabetização, Diversidade e Inclusão* (Department of Lifelong Learning, Literacy, Diversity and Inclusion)
Seedco   Structured Employment Economic Development Corporation
SENARC   *Secretaria Nacional de Renda de Cidadania* (National Department of Citizen's Income)
UFT   United Federation of Teachers
UnB   *Universidade de Brasília* (University of Brasília)
UNDP   United Nations Development Program
UNESCO   United Nations Educational, Scientific and Cultural Organization
UNICEF   United Nations Children's Fund
US   United States of America
UPZs   *Unidades de Planeamiento Zonal* (Units of Zoning Planing)

LIST OF FIGURES

LIST OF TABLES

Introduction

This book is about a magic silver bullet in the policy world: the renowned "Conditional Cash Transfers" (CCTs). It is about how they became a unanimous policy recommendation in a timespan of ten years. The book will examine what promises CCTs have and have not delivered, especially in the field of education, and what potential they could still bear, depending on how much political support they still have.[1]

For starters, conditional cash transfers are public programs that deliver cash directly to poor families, provided that they perform a set of predefined activities that are expected to reduce their condition of poverty—and especially of their children—in the long run. The delivery of cash is aimed at immediate poverty and hunger reduction, at the same time that the so-called conditionalities aim at breaking the intergenerational cycle of poverty.

An appraisal prepared for this book indicates that between 1994 and 2016, there were a total of 75 conditional cash transfer programs in the world. They span three continents—Africa, the Americas, and Asia—and are present in 40 countries. Having been adopted for different reasons and with some small variations, all of them are cash-based and conditional upon the completion of some education-related activity.

Different from other books on the same topic, this book is not a meta-analysis of various other studies, or a quantitative evaluation of a set of cases. It attempts to bring the story around CCTs, how they diffused to all corners of the world, and how some central and local governments implemented them. To some extent, the book is about the lived reality of a policy experience, one that has become world famous and whose future may be debatable at this point.

Not least important, this book is also about the international rise of the poverty-reduction agenda and how education has been intertwined with it in the wake of conditional cash transfers. It is about the astonishing international diffusion of CCTs and the various ways to explain it. It is also about the intriguing long life of these programs in most countries and how their political survival may not be related to how they spread in the first place. It is finally about their blurry future, as the poverty-reduction agenda may be giving space to more conservative and economic-focused agendas in various countries.

Finally, the book brings details about the policy trajectories of three CCT programs from different parts of the Americas: *Bolsa Familia* from Brazil; *Subsidios* from Bogota, Colombia and Opportunity NYC from New York, USA. Why these programs? Because each had a different take in terms of how they addressed education and related it to poverty reduction. Each tells us a different story in terms of how much education there is in conditional cash transfers. *Bolsa Familia*, with the "traditional" CCT design, only requires beneficiary families to send their children to school and maintain minimum attendance. *Subsidios*, having been designed and implemented by Bogota's Department of Education, went a little further and required graduation and even enrollment in higher education in some cases. Opportunity NYC, in turn, tried an ambitious design and went so far as to condition cash disbursements to performance improvement in school tests.

Each in a different way, these programs tried to impact education, either from the outside or from the inside, ultimately aiming to raise the education level of poor children as a measure to prevent that they grow into poor adults. The real design and implementation experiences related to the three programs are hidden treasures that are not visible if one only looks at the macrodata. This book hence brings the unique possibility of zooming out and in to better understand the policy world of CCTs in the past 20 years.

The first chapter begins by presenting the international rise of the poverty-reduction agenda in the broader development framework and how education was related to it. Then it moves to presenting the meaning of conditional cash transfer programs, when and where they were first created, telling the story of how they became internationally popular in the wake of the poverty-reduction agenda.

Chapter 2 brings a new and updated appraisal of all ever-existing CCTs with education-related conditions. It points to how they diffused over time and space, gradually being adopted by an increasing number of countries. The chapter lays down an overview of the most common characteristics of CCTs across the globe, looking at variables such as source of funding, education-related conditionalities, and program duration. The chapter also presents alternative theories that may help us explain CCT's worldwide diffusion.

Chapter 3 paves the way for the study of specific CCT cases, where the interest lies mainly in analyzing how CCTs and education policies have interrelated. The chapter briefly introduces the theories and concepts that framed the study of cases. It also explains the methodology used in the comparative study, so as to establish the credibility of its results.

Chapter 4 brings a complete account of the design, implementation, and frustrating results of Opportunity NYC, a conditional cash transfer program that was experimented in New York, supposedly following the example of the Mexican CCT. It tells how Opportunity NYC had a rationale that was distinct from any other CCT in the world, how it was financed only with private money, and how it was terminated after only three years of implementation. Finally, the chapter looks into the policy diffusion processes involving the program, revealing how it was not really the result of emulation from Mexico and how, even before its evaluation was completed, the program was being used as an international example.

Chapter 5 brings up the story of a not so prominent and yet very promising conditional cash transfer: the *Subsidios* program. It was adopted by Bogota's city government and, throughout its short life, combined characteristics that, from an educational perspective, make of it a very interesting case. The chapter also reveals how the political dynamics between Bogota's government and Colombia's national government restricted the international promotion of the program, even by the international development bank that had lent the money for its creation.

Chapter 6 is about the Brazilian *Bolsa Familia*, the largest conditional cash transfer program in the world. *Bolsa Familia* currently reaches 14 million families, including 17 million students. It has been one of the main contributors to the stark reduction of extreme poverty and to the elimination of hunger in Brazil over recent years. The chapter gives an account of how the program was created, how it currently works, and how it relates to education policies and practices in Brazil. The chapter also raises questions about the program's political survival, given the recent and abrupt changes in Brazil's political system.

Chapter 7 contrasts case-specific findings, pointing out what they reveal in terms of CCT's linkage (or absence of) to education policies and practices. Some suggested inputs to existing theories are provided, along with the presentation of some lessons learned. The findings are meant to inspire the large array of stakeholders that have somehow got involved in the CCT debate and expansion throughout the world. It speaks especially to those who have high hopes of CCTs having deeper impacts on the education indicators of developing countries and points out the challenges that need to be surmounted if those hopes are to become true. Lastly, the chapter is also dedicated to looking at CCT's long program lives. It argues that when funding is not an issue, most of these programs have been able to survive for long periods of time. *Bolsa Família* has existed since 2004 in Brazil and the same long life story applies to the multiplicity of CCTs in Latin America, such as in Chile, Ecuador, Uruguay, and even the national Colombian CCT.

Despite its history of long existence, the last and concluding chapter raises questions about CCTs' future. As the political thermometer changes from progressive to conservative in various countries, one cannot but wonder what will happen to the international poverty-reduction agenda, which brings us back to the discussions presented in the beginning of the book. As conservative governments come to power—whether legitimately or illegitimately—and as national budgets become tighter, it is not too clear if the poverty-reduction agenda, which made room for the creation and diffusion of CCTs, will remain as a top international development priority.

NOTE

1. This book builds on the author's doctoral dissertation and extends it, incorporating further data collection and analysis, especially new facts and developments occurred since 2010. See Morais de Sa e Silva, M. (2010). *Conditional cash transfers and education: United in theory, divorced in policy.* Unpublished doctoral dissertation, Columbia University, New York City.

PART I

A Best Practice to Reduce Present and Future Poverty

CHAPTER 1

Conditional Cash Transfer Programs and the Poverty-Reduction Agenda

Reducing poverty has never been an easy task, especially for poor families by themselves. However, it has not been an easy task for governments either, particularly those that have made the political decision to reduce or even eliminate from their societies the experience of living in poor conditions. Conditional cash transfers—or CCTs, as they have become known—have been spearheaded as a good policy solution for the plight of economic poverty. The CCT model carries the core idea that poverty will be alleviated immediately through the direct transfer of cash to poor families, which in return will have to perform a set of activities that are expected to reduce the chance that their children will grow into poor adults.

On the one hand, this core idea is the consequence of a perceived failure, across countries, of social work services that had been based on individual case management and the provision of social assistance services. Especially in developing countries, food subsidies that had been used to alleviate poverty and hunger had also proven ineffective and regressive—that is, as food subsidies were not exclusively for the poor, they tended to actually benefit those who purchased more, and not less food.

On the other hand, as CCTs first emerged in the 1990s, the combination of human capital ideas with that of human development led to a program architecture that sought to build human capital for future generations, and therefore attempted to break the intergenerational cycle of poverty.

© The Author(s) 2017
M. Morais de Sá e Silva, *Poverty Reduction, Education, and the Global Diffusion of Conditional Cash Transfers*, DOI 10.1007/978-3-319-53094-9_1

However, before CCTs conquered the world as an epidemic, it had not been always too obvious how poverty could be reduced in a sustainable manner. It had also not been too obvious that governments should invest public resources (or taxpayer money, if you will) in the improvement of living conditions of only a part of a country's population—actually a part that earns less and consequently pays less in taxes.

During my childhood in a small town in the interior of Brazil, my teachers would tell us that our country was among the most unequal in the world; that poverty was a structural problem derived from our colonial past. The way they taught transmitted a sense of utmost hopelessness. And yet, during my adult life, I saw poverty and inequality indicators being reduced everywhere in the country as the national CCT program—*Bolsa Familia*—began to be progressively implemented and strengthened.

This chapter tells the story of how the poverty-reduction agenda emerged and how conditional cash transfers became its most celebrated—if not only—policy solution.

1.1   THE INTERNATIONAL RISE OF THE POVERTY-REDUCTION AGENDA AND THE PLACE OF EDUCATION

As Kingdon (1995) tells us, problems do not automatically get included into the policy agenda, no matter how dire they may be or look. They need to be socially and politically recognized as problems, legitimate alternatives need to be available to solve them, and windows of opportunity have to emerge in order for governments to dedicate public policies to work around them. So even though poverty has always been a problem in every country, especially in those once labeled as the Third World, it was not until recently that poverty reduction became recognized as a policy issue.

The international rise of CCTs is hence fundamentally related to how poverty-reduction gained a central place in international and national policy agendas. Although the idea and discourse on "underdevelopment" arose after the speech by US President Harry Truman in 1949,[1] international concern for the world's poor arose only decades later. In the post-World War years, the pursuit of development was the first priority that was sought both nationally and internationally, particularly within the broader framework of the Cold War dispute. National governments and international organizations were for various decades focused on achieving greater development, under the fundamental assumption that economic growth would eventually trickle down and improve everyone's lives. Modernization theories, which significantly inspired most of the developmental thinking and action until the 1960s (Peet and Hartwick 2009), gave rise to development policies and international cooperation for development to be mostly concentrated on building infrastructures for a late Industrial Revolution. Industrialization and modernization were seen as prerequisites for everything else and, only when they had been finally achieved would there be growth in the gross domestic product (GDP), with some possibility for redistribution.

Modernization theories inspired policies based on the assumption that the Third World should emulate the development path taken by rich countries, in the hope that they could, therefore, also become "civilized". Poverty and inequality were then considered as symptoms of technological and economic backwardness, which would, on the one hand, be naturally removed once development had been achieved. On the other hand, the idea also prevailed that poverty and inequality would never be remediated without industrial progress. As development thinking was greatly influenced by orthodox economic thinking at the time, all aspects of life were second to economic wealth.

As that basic assumption seemed not to hold and as countries were taking "too long" to achieve economic development, some attention began to be increasingly paid to the idea of "basic needs" during the 1970s and 1980s. In 1976, the International Labor Organization (ILO) organized the World Employment Conference, in which governments, employers, and workers committed for the first time to the fulfillment of basic needs.

Interestingly, it was during the late Robert McNamara years at the World Bank that the idea of assuring people with fulfillment of basic needs became even more prominent. McNamara had been the United States (US) Defense Secretary who engineered the bulk of the war efforts in Vietnam. After he left—or was ousted from—his position in the US government and was appointed World Bank President, he increasingly implemented lending policies geared toward satisfying the needs of the developing world. According to the World Bank (2016), "he devised strategies to address specific needs: literacy, nutrition, reduction in infant mortality, and health. McNamara's obsession to assist those in 'absolute poverty' remained the backbone of his presidential tenure."

McNamara's attention to basic needs was furthered, although in a much more comprehensive and theory-backed manner, by the adoption of the human development approach by the United Nations Development Program (UNDP). This approach was materialized in the Human Development Index (HDI) and its corresponding annual Human Development Reports. The human development approach was based on Amartya Sen's concept of human capabilities and his vision of "development as freedom" (Sen 1999).

Led by Pakistani economist Mahbubul Haq, the creation of the HDI in 1990 marked the adoption of new and world-renowned metrics for development. For decades, GDP-based measures had served as the only standard for the definition and monitoring of development. Hence, the adoption of the HDI meant that not only would GDP be considered, but also education and health-related indicators. Such an expansion of the definition of development, giving centrality to its human aspects, was a first and important breakthrough toward putting poverty-reduction into the agenda. According to UNDP (2016), "Human development—or the human development approach—is about expanding the richness of human life, rather than simply the richness of the economy in which human beings live. It is an approach that is focused on people and their opportunities and choices."

The inclusion of education indicators—first adult literacy rates and then years of schooling—also gave a new impetus to putting education policies at the center of the policy agenda, with a direct link to the promotion of development. Linkages between education and development had always been a common assumption, especially as a result of human capital theories, which emerged in the 1960s. As human capital's main scholar, Schultz (1961) was the first to propose that, besides economic capital, human capital was also significant for productivity improvements and economic growth. However, in his framework, education was a means for the accumulation of capital, and not for the expansion of human capabilities. Hence, the human development approach was also important in giving a new role to education in the production function of development.

It should also be noted that the adoption of the human development approach came after developing countries had experienced widespread economic and social crises in the 1980s. These countries faced debt crisis and hyperinflation years that resulted from a long period of benevolent international lending, financed by petrodollars. After international resources dried up and interest rates were raised, some countries defaulted on their debt, while others had to borrow from international financial institutions, such as the World Bank and the International Monetary Fund (IMF). As these institutions rescued indebted countries, they also established a menu of policy conditions to be followed, which became best known as "the Washington Consensus" (Williamson 1989). These policy conditions guided the implementation of structural adjustment programs in borrowing countries, mostly following a neoliberal agenda.

However, structural adjustment came at a high social cost for many countries. As many of them had to adopt tight fiscal policies and mostly cut down on social expenditures, social services and welfare were reduced. All these combined with the contexts of economic crisis and inflation, resulted in the poor to suffer the most. Back then in Brazil, it was common to see images of street children and starving people on national television.

This scenario of increased world poverty, combined with a progressively expanded vision of development, allowed for the inclusion of poverty as a real and priority problem in the developing world. As a result, in the early 2000s, both the IMF and the World Bank started working with a new lending instrument called 'Poverty Reduction Strategy Papers' (PRSPs), where governments had to explicitly devise poverty-reduction programs in order to get additional loans approved. To this date, PRSPs or simply PRS (poverty reduction strategy) are tools used by the banks: "Poverty Reduction Strategies (PRS) are central to IMF-supported economic and financial programs in low-income countries. PRS documents assess poverty challenges, describe how macroeconomic, structural, and social policies and programs can promote growth and reduce poverty, and outline external financing needs and the associated sources of financing" (IMF 2016).

One should notice that it was also during those years that "the poor" actually arose as a defined group for targeted policy consideration. Until then, most governments had worked with the assumption that economic growth would produce positive spillover effects on the whole society, eventually benefiting those in the inferior income tiers. Other terminologies were then common, such as low-income, illiterate, unemployed, and out-of-school. However, the adoption of the poverty label allowed policymakers to encapsulate a number of social issues under the same terminology and within a single group.

Additionally, as poverty-reduction became an important part of the policy agenda, there was an increased need to target policies specifically at those considered to be "the poor," hence maximizing the resources and potential effects on poverty alleviation. But a first and important task in this process was the definition of who and where the poor were. Consequently, international and national statistics agencies invested efforts in defining how many were a country's poor. The basic concept behind that exercise was the definition of a poverty line, which is an income threshold below which families were to be considered poor or extremely poor. Some consider the poverty line the income-based measure for the idea of basic needs. Basically, the effort of defining the money value of a poverty line involves defining what those basic needs are on a daily basis and how much they cost.

Since 1990, the World Bank and international experts had worked on defining a standard international poverty line. For years, that line was defined as $1 in purchase power parity, mostly known as the one-dollar-a-day poverty line. Then in 2005 the World Bank revised world prices and raised the line to $1.25. Recently, in 2015, a new revision took place and the international poverty line is now at $1.90 a day (World Bank 2015).

Besides these efforts toward more accurate definitions and measurements, the end of the 1990s and the beginning of 2000s were also marked by the first international commitments toward the establishment of common global goals. In education, the Dakar Framework for Action was extensively negotiated during the 2000 World Education Forum and led to the first-ever agreed goals for education in every country: the Education for All goals (EFA). The EFA goals consisted of six simple and straightforward goals that aimed at some basic, although very significant improvements in terms of greater access and better quality of education by 2015. Responsibility for monitoring progress toward the achievement of the EFA goals was attributed to the United Nations Educational, Scientific and Cultural Organization (UNESCO), which since then has annually published the EFA Reports.

Concurrently, the United Nations member states gathered at the Millennium Summit in 2000 and approved the Millennium Development Goals, commonly known as the MDGs. Having 2015 also as their deadline, the MDGs comprised of eight goals, the first being to eradicate extreme poverty and hunger and the second to achieve universal primary education. This was not only an unprecedented multilateral move toward goal setting, it also represented the primacy of the social dimensions of development.

On the one hand, there was much concern at the time that the MDGs would overshadow the EFA goals, especially in terms of visibility, funding, and policy focus. On the other hand, the MDGs reinforced the idea that poverty went hand in hand with lack of education and that the poverty-reduction agenda should also involve efforts in the field of education. Hence, as poverty took an increasingly prominent place in the world development agenda, it brought education closely with it.

Since then, a number of organizations have been created with the explicit mandate of fighting, funding, or analyzing poverty worldwide. These are the cases of the United Nations International Policy Center, created in 2004, initially called the International Poverty Center. Also, in 2003 universities and research centers created a consortium to form the Abdul Latif Jameel Poverty Action Lab, whose main office is at the Massachusetts Institute of Technology (MIT) in the United States. Other organizations, in turn, have reoriented their work plans, so as to focus on poverty reduction. That is the case of the World Bank, which has adopted the motto "Working for a World Free of Poverty."

However, one should be clear that the international "poverty-reduction act" was not—and has not been—mainly formed by grassroots social movements or those who have actually experienced poverty. As the issue got included in the development agenda, discussions have been mostly led by economists and researchers trained in statistics, methods of randomization, and controlled trials. Somewhere along the way, poverty was turned into a technical matter, one that could be objectively measured, tested, and changed by means of planned interventions. In the policy sciences, the poverty-reduction agenda coincided with the strengthening of evidence-based policymaking. Educational specialists, particularly those without an economics background, have not actually participated much in the poverty-reduction core discussions and policymaking. As it will be later discussed in this book, the link between education and poverty-reduction has been most explored from a cost–benefit perspective, without much attention to quality issues or to what goes inside the "education black-box."

Interestingly, although not contingent upon it, the almost 20 years of the poverty-reduction agenda since the late 1990s have coincided with the election of left-leaning governments in various countries, especially in Latin America. For those governments' political agendas, it was not only technically but also politically and ideologically important to fight poverty and inequality. And as they were presented with a solution in the form of conditional cash transfers, most of them joined the "CCT wave."

1.2   THE RISE OF THE CONDITIONAL CASH TRANSFER MODEL

During the late 1990s and early 2000s, national and local governments had included poverty-reduction in their policy agendas. That was partially a consequence of international trends, but also a political consequence of the direct mobilization of interest groups and social movements that had been pressing their governments for policies toward better living conditions. Various pilot projects and programs were tried out, but there was one type of program that caught the attention of policymakers, as it had started producing results in Mexico and in some Brazilian cities: conditional cash transfers (CCTs).

Although there is not much evidence of cross-fertilization among those first CCT experiences—and they did not carry that label back then—those first programs were rather similar in their basic rationale: delivering cash directly to families, instead of subsidizing food or social services. As a payback, poor beneficiary families would have to perform some predefined activities that were considered important for development.

There is much controversy about which one may have been the very first CCT to be created. Two local programs from Brazil dispute such a title: *Bolsa Escola*, implemented in the country's federal district; and the Guarantee of Minimum Family Income, implemented by the city government of Campinas. Both the programs were initiated in early 1995 and were later scaledup to the national level, forming the National *Bolsa Escola* program in 2001.

The creation of the Guarantee of Minimum Family Income in Campinas, Brazil, was inspired by the Brazilian Senator, Eduardo Suplicy, who in 1991 had proposed the first bill to create a Citizen's Basic Income in Brazil. Behind the concept of a basic or minimum income is the "perception that all citizens should have the right to participate in the wealth of a nation" (Suplicy 2008, p. 5). Thus, it is not based on the idea of reducing poverty, but rather sharing the country's resources to make sure that every citizen has the minimum means of subsistence. According to Suplicy's first proposal, every Brazilian aged 25 and more and with a monthly income of less than US$150 would be entitled to a cash transfer corresponding to 30% of the difference between his income and the US$150 threshold. The resulting program should hence be unconditional and universal.

Also in 1991, Suplicy presented his ideas at a conference of economists and met Professor José Márcio Camargo. The professor agreed with his arguments, but added the idea that beneficiaries should be required to send their children to school, so as to simultaneously tackle the problem of child labor and out-of-school children in the country. Camargo publicized his proposal in a series of opinion editorials published in one of Brazil's largest newspapers—*Folha de São Paulo*—in 1991 and 1993.

Although Senator Suplicy belongs to the Workers' Party (PT), his ideas were influential enough to inspire the creation of the Campinas program by a municipal administration belonging to another party—the Brazilian Social Democratic Party (PSDB). The mayor of Campinas also adopted Camargo's suggestion and made the program conditional upon children's school attendance.

As for *Bolsa Escola*, its origins are linked to the Center for Contemporary Brazilian Studies at the University of Brasilia (Aguiar and Araújo 2002). The concept of a program that would provide monetary support to poor families so that they could send their children to school emerged out of discussions at the Center, which was then chaired by Cristovam Buarque,[2] currently Senator for the Federal District. In his 1994 book—*A Revolução nas Prioridades* (The Revolution in Priorities)—Buarque argued that education should be Brazil's first priority. He proposed various strategies to improve education in the country, the second being a "minimum income for each family with children in school" (Buarque 1994, p. 157). Consequently, as soon as Buarque took office as Governor of the Federal District in January 1995, he immediately created *Bolsa Escola* as one of his education policies.

The *Bolsa Escola* program in the Federal District was targeted at families whose monthly per capita income was below half a minimum wage and who lived in the region called Paranoá (Yonemura 2005). The program transferred one minimum salary per family per month (100 reais in 1995), regardless of the number of children in the household. That measure was meant to encourage family planning. In order to avoid migration from other parts of the country to the Federal District, the program also required beneficiary families to demonstrate a minimum of five years of local residency.

Odd as it may seem, there was no direct connection between the creation of the Campinas program and the one in the Federal District. Behind them were two core figures in the Brazilian Workers' Party at the time—Senator Eduardo Suplicy and former Governor Cristovam Buarque—but they had very distinct ideas about what their programs were supposed to mean. As a matter of fact, Aguiar and Araújo (2002) argue that there is "a great strategic gap between the two programs" (pp. 41–42). According to them, "the priority target public of the program in Campinas is typically related to the area of social aid, while *Bolsa Escola* basically benefits those who attend school" (p. 41). Evidence of that difference is the fact that *Bolsa Escola* was managed by the Federal District's Department of Education, whereas the Guarantee of Minimum Family Income was housed at Campinas' Department of Family, Children, Adolescents and Social Action (Yonemura 2005).

Internationally, *Bolsa Escola* became more widely known than the Campinas program. In part, this may be related to its emphasis on education. On the other hand, it may also have to do with the fact that international organizations such as the UNESCO and the United Nations Children's Fund (UNICEF) have their country offices in Brasilia, where *Bolsa Escola* was first implemented. International support to *Bolsa Escola* came in the form of the UNICEF award "Children and Peace" in 1996, various UNESCO publications about the program, and verbal recommendations at international meetings, such as that by UN Secretary General Kofi Annan in a 2000 speech (Aguiar and Araújo 2002).

Regardless of their motivation and underlying philosophy, the fact is that both *Bolsa Escola* and the Campinas program consisted of monetary transfers made to poor families on the condition that their children were enrolled in school and maintained minimum attendance. This model, which was later labeled by the international community as "conditional cash transfers," immediately caught the attention of other states and municipalities in Brazil.[3] In 1997, four other states had similar programs and six were discussing their adoption (Coelho 2008).

Meanwhile, both Senators Suplicy and then Governor Buarque made efforts to convince President Fernando Henrique Cardoso to create a national CCT. In 1996, Senator Suplicy arranged for a meeting between the President and Belgian philosopher Philippe van Parijs, who authored the book "Arguing for basic income: Ethical foundations for a radical reform." Van Parijs argued that the ideal would be to create a universal and unconditional basic income policy, but that in the meantime it would be positive to start with a targeted, conditional transfer program (interviewee C13). Governor Buarque wrote various letters to the President and to then Minister of Education Paulo Renato de Souza, who initially rejected the proposal of nationalizing the *Bolsa Escola* experience (interviewee C15).

However, there was such a widespread local interest in the CCT model that in 1997 the President approved the provision of financial support to municipalities that were willing to create their own programs. Similar to the Campinas program, whose government belonged to the President's party, the federal support initiative was named Guarantee of Minimum Family Income Program. At first, the federal government provided only financial support to municipalities that were in a priority list according to pre-established criteria. Of over 5000 municipalities, 1150 received federal funding and were able to create their municipal CCTs (Coelho 2008).

Due to suspicions of corruption and malfunctioning problems, the federal program was terminated in 2000 (Coelho 2008). However, since it was very popular and municipalities continued to press for financial support in order to maintain their local CCTs, in 2001 the federal government approved the "National Minimum Income Program linked to Education—*Bolsa Escola.*" As the name indicates, it was a hybrid of the original CCTs developed in Campinas and in the Federal District. Additionally, this new program, which came to be known as the "Federal *Bolsa Escola,*" introduced two important changes compared to its federal predecessor: a greater education focus and scale. The program also had some relevant differences compared to previous local CCTs: transfer amounts were defined in terms of the number of children (maximum of three) and were set at 15 reais per child/per month. Consequently, the maximum transfer amount was 45 reais, which corresponded to only 25% of the minimum wage at the time (180 reais). That represented a significant reduction in payment amounts, which were of one full minimum wage in the local *Bolsa Escola*, for instance.

Besides *Bolsa Escola*, Brazil's Federal Government at the time also created other sector-based cash transfer programs, such as *Bolsa Alimentação* (food grant) and *Vale Gás* (cooking gas coupon). These programs did not bring education conditionalities, but were equally based on the direct delivery of cash from the Federal government to beneficiary families. In 2003, in the first year of President Lula's first term, he made the decision to merge the cash transfer programs into a single CCT, now called the *Bolsa Família* (family grant). A later chapter of this book is entirely dedicated to presenting *Bolsa Família* and the various incremental changes that have been made to the program implementation to date. As of 2016, *Bolsa Família* is the largest CCT program in the world, benefiting over 14 million families.

Interestingly, Brazil's first two programs—*Bolsa Escola* and Guarantee of Minimum Family Income—seem to have been designed and implemented almost on a combination of long-nurtured policy ideas and strong political will. The use of program and policy evaluation techniques or experimentation was not a widespread practice at the time. Hence, these programs were put in place and later scaledup because there was a strong public perception that they made a lot of sense and were the right things to do vis-à-vis the high poverty levels in the country at the time.

In 1997, the Brazilian programs were joined by a new and prominent-to-be CCT in Mexico: *Progresa*[4], which was renamed *Oportunidades* in 2002 and *Prospera* in 2014. Different from the first Brazilian experiences, *Progresa* was born as a national program, one that came to replace food subsidy programs. Also, *Progresa* first targeted Mexico's rural population and only years later got to be scaledup to urban centers. Different from *Bolsa Escola,* which had mostly an educational focus, *Progresa* was conceived as a poverty reduction program. To date, it is probably the most well-known CCT in the world, to the effect that it came to somewhat inspire the creation of a similar program in New York City, which carried the name Opportunity NYC (see Chap. 4).

From the outset, this kind of program carried an underlying set of assumptions: (1) giving cash directly to the poor was considered more effective than the provision of subsidies or social assistance; (2) it was not acceptable to just give money to the poor without asking them for something in return; and (3) there was a need to assure that those families would eventually overcome poverty and no longer need government cash—education and health-related activities could work in liberating the families from the poverty trap. In international parlance, CCTs were able to alleviate extreme poverty while breaking the intergenerational poverty cycle.

However, to be fair, the credit for the first CCT program with an educational component should actually go to Bangladesh's Female Secondary School Assistance Program (FSSAP). It was created in 1994 (a year before Brazil's CCTs) through a World Bank loan and consisted of the payment of stipends and tuition to girls living in poor areas and who had completed Grade 5. According to Bhatnagar et al. (2003) , the program coresponsibilities were: "attend school for at least 75% of the school year; obtain at least 45% marks on average in final examinations; and remain unmarried through completion of SSC" (p. 3). Bangladesh's FSSAP was expected to tackle the very low education level of girls in the country and was, from the beginning, a CCT with an education—rather than a poverty reduction—objective. That is likely to be the reason that most books and studies of CCTs overlook its existence.

As the variety of poverty reduction and social programs expanded, so did the terminology around them. Bangladesh's FSSAP, for instance, would be nowadays considered a "labeled cash transfer" (Benhassine et. al 2015), for its focus on covering educational expenses. There are also social cash transfers, which broadly correspond to unconditional transfers. Of a similar unconditional nature are the noncontributory pensions, which are generally aimed at the low-income, elderly, and disabled persons, usually being paid for life. Cash transfers, conditional or not, may carry the name of grants, stipends, or subsidies. Besides cash transfers, there are also in-kind transfers, especially in the form of food—such as school-feeding programs—and the donation of livestock. In some countries, in-kind transfers have been made conditional, as in the case of school-feeding programs that are conditional upon a minimum level of class attendance.

Even *The Economist*, an openly liberal magazine, which trusts government action very little, has recognized the value and world diffusion of CCTs: "The programmes have spread because they work. They cut poverty. They improve income distribution. And they do so cheaply" (*The Economist* 2010). As in the case of various international models, CCTs around the world retain a core set of characteristics, which remains unchanged from country to country; they are targeted only at poor families, are based on direct cash delivery, and have human capital-related conditions, most of them in terms of education and health. Consequently, variation across programs has mostly occurred around the following issues (and so has most of the debate and research work):

1. Targeting criteria.
2. Targeting mechanisms.
3. Conditions and how to verify their accomplishment.

4. Targeting criteria.
5. Payment amounts.
6. Payment method.
7. Duration of benefits.

As CCTs evolved and spread, a number of scholars, researchers, and institutions started concentrating efforts on studying, analyzing, and evaluating them. Actually, CCTs are probably among the most studied, researched, and evaluated policy models. For every CCT program there is a set of papers and program evaluations, most of them carried out from a quantitative and econometrics perspective, often trying to measure impact. Many of them are randomized controlled trials that compare different schemes (in terms of transfer amounts, conditionalities, and implementation processes) against a control group.

In fact, some CCT programs were actually designed and implemented as an experiment, especially the most recent experiences in Africa (i.e., Morocco). Bogota and NYC are also two clear examples of it. The ethical implications of social policy experimentation are certainly up for discussion. For instance, although experiments are supposed to advance science and evidence-based policymaking, they have a real impact on beneficiaries' lives, especially if the experiment does not become a public policy. It also has impacts on the mobilization of government resources, as personnel and institutions are mobilized to test programs that will eventually be discontinued.

Also, in various cases, experiments have been designed and evaluated by foreign scholars and researchers on contract, who eventually have the benefit of writing academic papers to present the achieved results. Certainly a very good deal for them, but not necessarily for the implementing countries. Interestingly enough, no one has ever followed up to assess the consequences of failed and discontinued trials. Additionally, one should ask: What has happened to evaluation results? Have they been used for decision-making? Have evaluation costs, incurred in the contracting of foreign scholars and consultants, been worth it?

As CCTs became central to policy and research agendas, poverty reduction became the link for the joint work of various sectors around CCTs. Having collaboration between institutions and actors of various policy areas is not an easy task and is still close to a mystery for policy analysts. However, the CCT model enabled governments to achieve exactly that: to have the fields of social work, education, and health working collaboratively. Why so against all the odds? First, because the three policy sectors recognized poverty-reduction as a common agenda, both politically and as an important shared goal for their respective sectors. Second, because CCTs did not demand each sector to alter significantly their ethos and individual objectives. Especially for the education and health sectors, CCTs did not bring much additional work and, as discussed later in this book, absolutely no real reform.

Hence, to some extent, the survival of the CCT policy model is directly related to the centrality of poverty reduction in the international policy agenda. Other policy goals, although not exclusive or contradictory to policy reduction, may compete for that agenda, such as economic growth—or the fight against economic recession—and sustainable development.

The following chapter will be dedicated to presenting the international diffusion of the CCT model, both across countries and through time. As the data suggest, this policy model has existed for over 20 years and could be at its height. Various theoretical approaches will be presented in order to provide for possible explanations of such an epidemic diffusion. Also, some analyses will be made as to how different countries have incorporated this cherished policy model.

NOTES

1. "We must embark on a bold new program for making the benefits of our scientific advances and industrial progress available for the improvement and growth of underdeveloped areas. More than half the people of the world are living in conditions approaching misery. Their food is inadequate. They are victims of disease. Their economic life is primitive and stagnant. Their poverty is a handicap and a threat both to them and to more prosperous areas" (Truman 1949).
2. CristovamBuarque is originally Professor of Economics at the University of Brasilia (UnB). Over the past twenty years he has been President of the University, Governor of the Federal District, Minister of Education, candidate for President of Brazil, and is currently Senator for the Federal District.
3. Brazil is a federation comprised by three autonomous levels of government: the union (federal government), states (26 plus the Federal District) and municipalities (5564). Each municipality has its own autonomous government, which is elected by direct popular vote. Additionally, municipalities can collect taxes and create their own laws in certain fields, provided

that they are compatible with state and federal laws and the Brazilian Constitution.

4. The name *Progresa* was somewhat of an acronym for Program of Education, Health and Food (*Programa de Educación, Salud y Alimentación*).

REFERENCES

Aguiar, M., & Araújo, C. H. (2002). *Bolsa Escola: Education to confront poverty.* Brasilia: UNESCO.

Benhassine, N., Devoto, F., Duflo, E., Dupas, P., & Pouliquen, V. (2015). Turning a shove into a nudge? A "Labeled Cash Transfer" for education. *American Economic Journal: Economic Policy, American Economic Association,* 7(3), 86–125.

Bhatnagar, D., Dewan, A., Moreno Torres, M., & Kanungo, P. (2003). *Female secondary school assistance program.* World Bank: Washington, DC.

Buarque, C. (1994). *A revolução nas prioridades: Da modernidade técnica à modernidade ética* [The revolution in priorities: From technical to ethical modernity]. São Paulo: Paz e Terra.

Coelho, D. B. (2008). *A difusão do programa Bolsa Escola: Competição política e inovação no setor social* [The diffusion of the *Bolsa Escola* Program: Political competition and innovation in the social sector]. Unpublished manuscript presented at XXXII Annual Meeting of the Brazilian National Association of Graduate Studies and Research in the Social Sciences (ANPOCS).

IMF. (2016). Poverty reduction strategy in IMF-supported programs. Retrieved July 14, 2016, from https://www.imf.org/external/np/exr/facts/prsp.htm.

Kingdon, J. (1995). *Agendas, alternatives, and public policies.* New York: Longman.

Peet, R., & Hartwick, E. (2009). *Theories of development: Contentions, arguments, alternatives.* New York: Guilford Press.

Sen, A. (1999). *Development as freedom* (1st ed.). New York: Oxford University Press.

Schultz, T. S. (1961). Investment in human capital. *The American Economic Review,* 51, 1–17.

Suplicy, E. M. (2008, June 20). *From the family scholarship program towards the citizen's basic income in Brazil.* Paper presented at the XII International Congress of the Basic Income Earth Network (BIEN), Dublin.

The Economist. (2010, July 29). *Give the poor money. Conditional-cash transfers are good. They could be even better.*

Truman, H. (1949). *Inaugural address.* Retrieved July 7, 2015, from http://www.trumanlibrary.org/whistlestop/50yr_archive/inagural20jan1949.htm.

UNDP. (2016). *About human development.* Retrieved July 13, 2016, from http://hdr.undp.org/en/humandev.

Williamson, J. (1989). What Washington means by policy reform. In J. Williamson (Ed.), *Latin American readjustment: How much has happened* (pp. 7–20). Washington: Institute for International Economics.

World Bank. (2015). *Global poverty line update*. Retrieved July 15, 2016, from http://www.worldbank.org/en/topic/poverty/brief/global-poverty-line-faq.

World Bank. (2016). *Robert Strange McNamara: 5th President of the World Bank Group (1968–1981)*. Retrieved July 11, 2016, from http://www.worldbank.org/en/about/archives/history/past-presidents/robert-strange-mcnamara.

Yonemura, A. (2005). *The changing social agenda in Brazil: An analysis of the policymaking process in the case of Bolsa Escola*. Unpublished doctoral dissertation, Teachers College, Columbia University.

CHAPTER 2

The International Diffusion of Conditional Cash Transfers

By 2009, Fiszbein and Schady (2009), in a comprehensive book on conditional cash transfers (CCT) experiences, counted 20 countries that by then had some sort of program of a CCT nature. A year later, Morais de Sa e Silva (2010) counted a total of 40 countries. Now repeating the same exercise, but considering a timeframe from 1994 to 2016, I have counted a current total of 47 programs in 40 countries, with a historic stock of 75 programs over that time period.[1]

The world is currently divided into 193 United Nations member states, including Palestine, Kosovo, Taiwan, Western Sahara, and Greenland. Beyond the country/state definition, the World Bank has identified 218 different economies in the world, among which 139 are considered low or middle income. Hence, a fifth of all countries have adopted some sort of CCT program. And if one excludes the United States from the count, almost a third of all low-income or middle-income economies have adopted the CCT solution. This is far from irrelevant in the policy world. When neoinstitutionalists, for instance, talk about the increasing policy isomorphism in education, they refer to general practices such as mandatory homework or girls' education (Baker and LeTendre 2005). However, how does one explain that when as many as 40 countries have bought into the specifics of a conditional cash transfer program?

CCT adoption was incremental and, to some extent, regionally oriented. It conformed to the epidemic model pointed out by Steiner-Khamsi (2006), according to whom policy diffusion occurs just like the

© The Author(s) 2017
M. Morais de Sá e Silva, *Poverty Reduction, Education, and the Global Diffusion of Conditional Cash Transfers*, DOI 10.1007/978-3-319-53094-9_2

spread of an epidemic, forming a lazy-S curve. If one plots the year when the programs were initiated in each country, the resulting curve is as shown in Graph 2.1.

In some countries, more than one program has been adopted, as there were different CCT programs at the national and local levels. Taking that into account, the total number of programs is even greater, as Table 2.1 indicates.

As Fig. 2.1 indicates, the very first programs were almost equally present in all the three continents—the Americas, Africa, and Asia. However, if one looks at Fig. 2.2, it is apparent that the CCT spread caught up faster in Latin America. Interestingly, CCT diffusion appears to have happened more intensively from 2005 to 2010, with the total number of CCT countries going from 9 in the year 2000 to 37 in 2010 (Fig. 2.3). In 2016, the total number of countries with a CCT program was 40, signaling toward a possible stabilization in CCT diffusion (see Fig. 2.4).

Equally interesting is how these programs have had relatively long lives, considering the "policy churn" (Hess 1999) that is so characteristic of developing countries. For instance, as many as eight programs have existed for 12 years, which in most places corresponds to three electoral cycles. And 30 of the 75 programs have existed for 10 years or more. Hence, in this case, the reasons for policy sustainability are as interesting

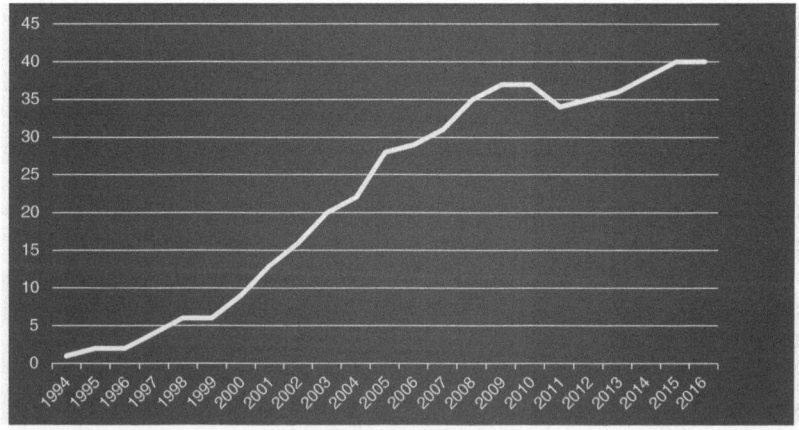

Graph 2.1   CCT diffusion per country (1994–2016)

Table 2.1 CCTs around the world (1994–2016)

Region	Country		Program	Beginning year	Ending year
Americas	1. Argentina	1	*Ciudadania Portena*	2005	Ongoing
		2	*Jefes de Hogar*	2002	2005
		3	*Familias por la Inclusión Social*	2005	2010
		4	*Asignacion Universal por Hijo para Protección Social*	2009	Ongoing
	2. Belize	5	Building Opportunities for Our Social Transformation (Boost)	2011	Ongoing
	3. Bolivia	6	*Bono Esperanza*	2003	2005
		7	*Bono Juancito Pinto*	2006	Ongoing
	4. Brazil	8	*Bolsa Escola*	1995	
		9	Guarantee of Minimum Family Income	1995	
		10	Program for the Eradication of Child Labor – PETI	1996	2006
		11	Federal Bolsa Escola	2001	2003
		12	*Bolsa Familia*	2003	Ongoing
	5. Chile	13	*Chile Solidario*	2002	2012
		14	*Ingreso Etico Familiar*	2012	Ongoing
	6. Colombia	15	*Más Familias en Accion*	2001	Ongoing
		16	*Subsidios Condicionados a la Asistencia Escolar*	2005	2012
	7. Costa Rica	17	*Superemonos*	2000	2002
		18	*Avancemos*	2006	Ongoing
	8. Dominican Republic	19	*Tarjeta de Asistencia Escolar*	2001	2004
		20	*Solidaridad*	2005	2012
		21	*Progresando con Solidaridad*	2012	Ongoing
	9. Ecuador	22	*Bono de Desarrollo Humano*	2003	Ongoing
	10. El Salvador	23	*Programa de Apoyo a Comunidades Solidarias en El Salvador* (previously *Red Solidaria*)	2005	Ongoing

(continued)

Table 2.1 (continued)

Region	Country		Program	Beginning year	Ending year
	11. Guatemala	24	Protección y Desarrollo de la Niñez y Adolescencia Trabajadora	2007	2008
		25	Mi Familia Progresa	2008	2011
		26	Mi Bono Seguro	2012	Ongoing
	12. Haiti	27	Ti Manman Cheri	2012	Ongoing
	13. Honduras	28	Programa de Asignacion Familiar	1998	2009
		29	Bono Vida Mejor	2010	Ongoing
	14. Jamaica	30	PATH	2001	Ongoing
	15. Mexico	31	*Oportunidades* (previously *Progresa*)	1997	2014
		32	*Prospera*	2014	Ongoing
	16. Nicaragua	33	*Red de Proteccion Social*	2000	2006
	17. Panama	34	*Red de Oportunidades*	2006	Ongoing
	18. Paraguay	35	*Tekopora*	2005	Ongoing
		36	*Abrazo*	2005	Ongoing
	19. Peru	37	*Juntos*	2005	Ongoing
	20. Uruguay	38	*Ingreso Ciudadano*	2005	2007
		39	*Asignaciones Familiares*	2008	Ongoing
	21. United States	40	Opportunity NYC	2007	2010
Asia and the Pacific	22. Bangladesh	41	Female Secondary School Assistance Program	1994	2008
		42	Primary Education Stipend Program	2002	Ongoing
		43	Reaching Out-of-School Children	2004	Ongoing
	23. Cambodia	44	Japan Fund for Poverty Reduction Girls Scholarship Program	2002	2005
		45	Cambodia Education Support Project	2005	Ongoing
	24. India	46	*Balika Samridhi Yojana*	1997	Ongoing
		47	Conditional Cash Transfer Scheme for Girl Child (*Dhanalakshmi*)	2008	Ongoing

(continued)

Table 2.1 (continued)

Region	Country		Program	Beginning year	Ending year
	25. Indonesia	48	*Jaring Pegamanan Social*	1998	2002
		49	*Keluarga Harapan*	2007	Ongoing
	26. Mongolia	50	Child Money Program	2005	2010
		51	Child Money Program	2012	Ongoing
	27. Pakistan	52	Participation in Education through Innovative Scheme for the Excluded Vulnerable	2003	2006
		53	Punjab Female School Stipend Program	2004	Ongoing
		54	Child Support Program	2006	Ongoing
	28. Philippines	55	Pantawid Pamilyang Pilipino Program (initially AHON)	2007	Ongoing
	29. Turkey	56	Social Risk Mitigation Project	2001	Ongoing
Middle East	30. Yemen	57	Basic Education Development Project	2004	2012
Africa	31. Burkina Faso	58	Nahouri Cash Transfers Pilot Project	2008	2010
	32. Congo	59	LISUNGI Safety Nets Project	2014	Ongoing
	33. Egypt	60	Ain el-Sira Project (Cairo)	2009	2011
		61	Takaful	2015	Ongoing
	34. Ghana	62	Livelihood Empowerment against Poverty	2008	Ongoing
	35. Guinea	63	Cash Transfer for Health, Nutrition and Education	2013	Ongoing
	36. Kenya	64	Cash Transfers for Orphans and Vulnerable Children	2004	Ongoing
	37. Madagascar	65	*Le Transfert Monétaire Conditionnel*	2014	Ongoing

(continued)

Table 2.1   (continued)

Region	Country		Program	Beginning year	Ending year
	38. Morocco	66	Morocco's Cash Transfer for Children (Tayssir Program)	2008	2010
		67	Direct Assistance to Widows in a Precarious Situation with Dependent Children	2015	Ongoing
	39. Mozambique	68	*Bolsa Escola*	2003	2006
	40. Namibia	69	Child Maintenance Grant	2000	Ongoing
	41. Nigeria	70	In Care of the Poor	2007	Ongoing
	42. Senegal	71	Conditional Cash Transfer for Orphans and Vulnerable Children	2008	Ongoing
		72	*Programme National de Bourses de Sécurité Familiale*	2013	Ongoing
	43. South Africa	73	CCT to Support Vulnerable Children in the Context of HIV/AIDS and Poverty	2005	Ongoing
	44. Tanzania	74	Community-based Conditional Cash Transfer	2009	Ongoing
	45. Tunisia	75	*Programme National d'Aide aux Familles Nécessiteuses*	2013	Ongoing

as the reasons for policy adoption. Also, as these programs have had relatively long lives and there is some indication of stabilization in their diffusion process (new adoptions are currently less frequent), one is likely to ask about what will happen next.

What else do we know about these 75 programs? As given in Table 2.2, there is an interesting story about actors and policy fields to be told. First, 42 of the 75 programs (56%) received some kind of foreign funding, ranging from bilateral donors to international financial institutions, like the World Bank and regional development banks. The World Bank alone was present in 29 of those partially or entirely

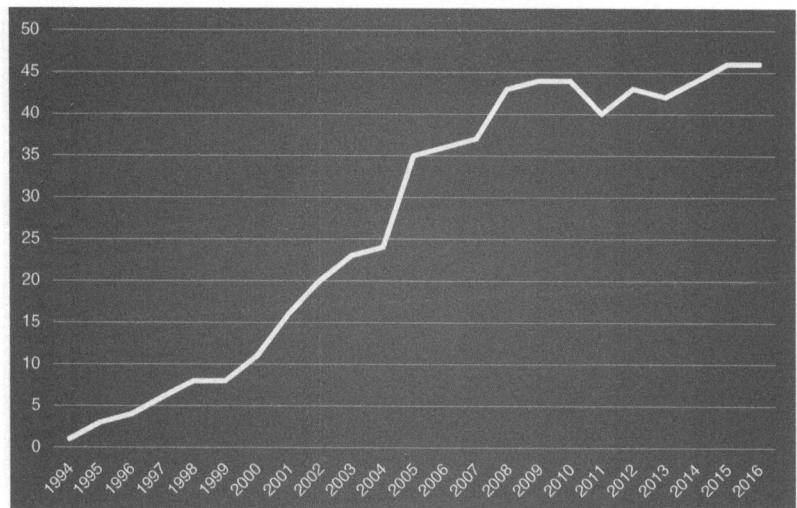

Graph 2.2 CCT diffusion—all programs (1994–2016)

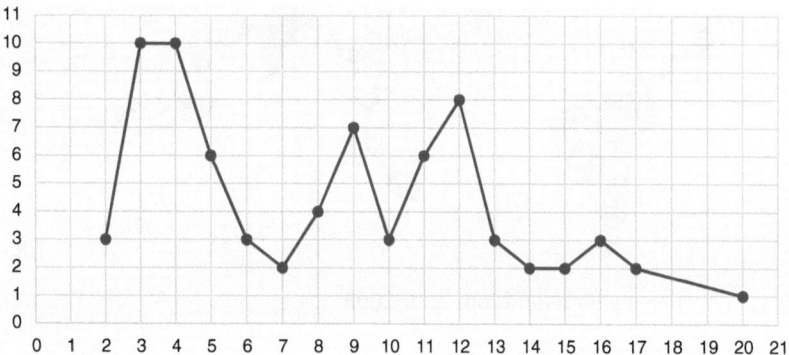

Graph 2.3 Frequency of years of program duration (1994–2016)

foreign-funded programs, which represents almost 40% of all programs. The international presence in the structuring and/or financing of CCT programs suggests that international actors have acted as important policy entrepreneurs for the adoption of the CCT model, and hence were an

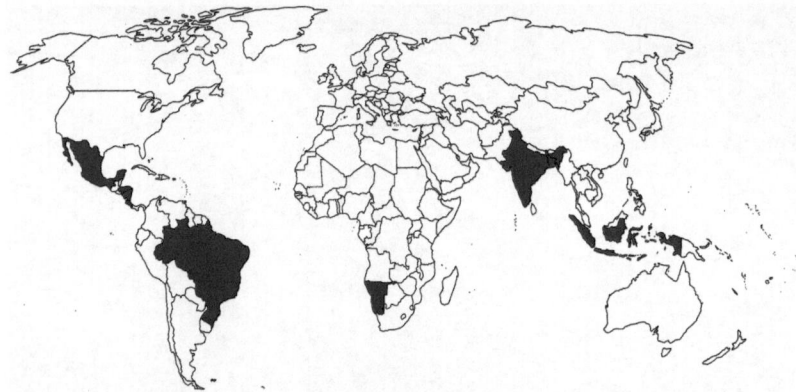

Fig. 2.1   Geographical diffusion—year 2000

Fig. 2.2   Geographical diffusion—year 2005

important part of the story behind their global diffusion. If one were to count the number of CCT studies and evaluations financed by bilateral donors, international banks, and other international organizations, the resulting number would be equally impressive.

Also apparent from Table 2.2 is how the majority of programs have limited their built-in conditions in education to school attendance only. In fact, that is the case in 49 of the 75 programs (65.3%). Some

Fig. 2.3 Geographical diffusion—year 2010

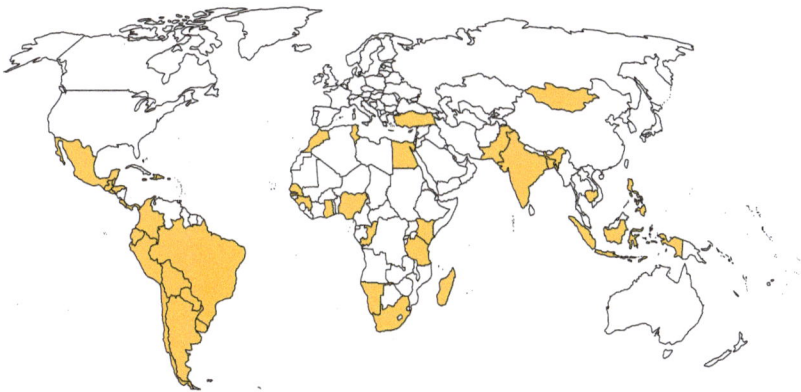

Fig. 2.4 Geographical diffusion—year 2015

interesting conclusions can be drawn from these numbers: (1) most programs have remained true to the first CCT experiences, such as those
in Mexico (*Progresa*) and Brazil (*Bolsa Escola*), whose only education-
related condition was school attendance; (2) there is an embedded perception that poverty goes hand-in-hand with lack of schooling, which
therefore means that access to education services should be a priority;
and (3) in the past 20-plus years of CCT existence, there has not been a

Table 2.2 Funding source and education-related condition

Region		Country	Program	Responsible government institution	Funding sources	Scope	Education-related condition
1. Argentina	1		Ciudadania Portena	Government of Buenos Aires	City government	City-wide	School attendance
	2		Jefes de Hogar	Ministry of Labor and Social Security	Central government and World Bank	National	School attendance
	3		Familias por la Inclusión Social	Ministry of Social Development	Central government and Interamerican Development Bank	National	School attendance
	4		Asignacion Universal por Hijo para Protección Social	Administración Nacional de la Seguridad Social	Central government	National	School attendance
2. Belize	5		Building Opportunities for Our Social Transformation (Boost)	Ministry of Human Development, Social Transformation and Poverty Alleviation	Central government	National	School attendance
3. Bolivia	6		Bono Esperanza	Government of El Alto	Municipal government	City-wide	School attendance
4. Brazil	7		Bono Juancito Pinto	Ministry of Education	Central government	National	School attendance
	8		Bolsa Escola	Government of the Federal District	State government	State	School attendance
	9		Guarantee of Minimum Family Income	Government of Campinas	City government	City-wide	School attendance
	10		Program for the Eradication of Child Labor — PETI	Ministry of Social Development and Fight Against Hunger	Central government	National	School attendance

(continued)

Table 2.2 (continued)

Region Country		Program	Responsible government institution	Funding sources	Scope	Education-related condition
	11	Federal *Bolsa Escola*	Ministry of Education	Central government	National	School attendance
	12	*Bolsa Familia*	Ministry of Social Development and Fight Against Hunger	Central government, supported by past loans from the World Bank and the Inter-American Development Bank (IDB)	National	School attendance
5. Chile	13	Chile Solidario	Ministry of Planning	Central government	National	Tailored conditionalities for each family
	14	Ingreso Etico Familiar	Ministry of Social Development	Central government	National	School attendance, school achievement and secondary school graduation
6. Colombia	15	Más Familias en Accion	Presidency of the Republic	Central government, World Bank and Interamerican Development Bank	National	School attendance
	16	Subsidios Condicionados a la Asistencia Escolar	Bogotá Department of Education	IDB and Department of Education	City-wide	Attendance, grade promotion, and secondary school graduation

(continued)

Table 2.2 (continued)

Region	Country		Program	Responsible government institution	Funding sources	Scope	Education-related condition
7. Costa Rica		17	Superemonos	Mixed Institute for Social Assistance	National Fund for Social Development and Interamerican Development Bank	National	School attendance
		18	Avancemos	Ministry of Housing and Social Development	Central government	National	Attendance and grade promotion
8. Dominican Republic		19	Tarjeta de Asistencia Escolar	State Secretariat for Education	Central government	National	School attendance and academic achievement
		20	Solidaridad	Social Policies Bureau	Central government and Interamerican Development Bank	National	School attendance
		21	Progresando con Solidaridad	Vice-Presidency	Central government	National	School attendance
9. Ecuador		22	Bono de Desarrollo Humano	Ministry of Economic and Social Inclusion	Central government, World Bank and Interamerican Development Bank	National	School attendance
10. El Salvador		23	Programa de Apoyo a Comunidades Solidarias en El Salvador (previously Red Solidaria)	Social Area at the President's Office	World Bank, Interamerican Development Bank and other donors	National	School attendance and graduation

(continued)

Table 2.2 (continued)

Region Country	Program	Responsible government institution	Funding sources	Scope	Education-related condition
11. Guatemala	24 Protección y Desarrollo de la Niñez y Adolescencia Trabajadora	Social Development Department at City Government	Municipal government and Italian cooperation	City-wide	School attendance and grade promotion
	25 Mi Familia Progresa	Ministry of Education	Central government and World Bank	National	School attendance
	26 Mi Bono Seguro	Ministry of Social Development	Central government	National	School attendance
12. Haiti	27 Ti Manman Cheri	Ministry of Economy and Finance	PetroCaribe/Venezuela Fund	National	School attendance
13. Honduras	28 Programa de Asignación Familiar	Presidency of the Republic	Central government and Interamerican Development Bank	National	School attendance
	29 Bono Vida Mejor	Presidency of the Republic	Central government, World Bank and Interamerican Development Bank	National	School attendance
14. Jamaica	30 PATH	Ministry of Labor and Social Security	World Bank	National	School attendance
15. Mexico	31 Oportunidades (previously Progresa)	Secretariat for Social Development	Central government and World Bank	National	School attendance and secondary school graduation

(continued)

Table 2.2 (continued)

Region	Country		Program	Responsible government institution	Funding sources	Scope	Education-related condition
		32	Prospera	National Coordination for Prospera, Secretariat for Social Development	Central government and World Bank	National	School attendance, secondary school graduation and enrolment in higher education
	16. Nicaragua	33	Red de Proteccion Social	Family Ministry	Central government and Interamerican Development Bank	National	School attendance
	17. Panama	34	Red de Oportunidades	Ministry of Social Development	Central government	National	School attendance
	18. Paraguay	35	Tekopora	Secretary of Social Action	Central government, World Bank, Interamerican Development Bank, and other donors	National	School attendance
		36	Abrazo	National Secretariat for Children and Adolescents	United Nations Childrens Fund	National	School attendance and grade promotion
	19. Peru	37	Juntos	Presidency of the Council of Ministers	Central government and Interamerican Development Bank	National	School attendance
	20. Uruguay	38	Ingreso Ciudadano	Ministry of Social Development	Central government	National	School enrollment
		39	Asignaciones Familiares	Ministry of Social Development	Central government	National	School attendance

(continued)

Table 2.2 (continued)

Region	Country		Program	Responsible government institution	Funding sources	Scope	Education-related condition
	21. United States	40	Opportunity NYC	City Department of Education and Center for Economic Opportunity	Various private sponsors	City-wide	School attendance and academic achievement
Asia and the Pacific	22. Bangladesh	41	Female Secondary School Assistance Program	Ministry of Education	Central Government, World Bank, Asian Development Bank, and other donors	National	School attendance and performance. Girls should remain unmarried
		42	Primary Education Stipend Program	Ministry of Education	Central government	National	School attendance
		43	Reaching Out-of-School Children	Ministry of Education	Central government and World Bank	National	School attendance and academic achievement
	23. Cambodia	44	Japan Fund for Poverty Reduction Girls Scholarship Program	Ministry of Education	Japan Fund for Poverty Reduction	National	Enrolment, attendance and grade promotion
		45	Cambodia Education Support Project	Ministry of Education	World Bank	National	Enrolment, attendance and grade promotion
	24. India	46	Balika Samridhi Yojana	Ministry of Women and Child Development	Central government	National	School attendance and girls should remain unmarried

(continued)

Table 2.2 (continued)

Region Country		Program	Responsible government institution	Funding sources	Scope	Education-related condition
	47	Conditional Cash Transfer Scheme for Girl Child (*Dhanalakshmi*)	Ministry of Women and Child Development	Central government	National	School attendance and girls should remain unmarried
25. Indonesia	48	Jaring Pegamanan Social		Central government and World Bank	National	School enrollment
	49	Keluarga Harapan	Ministry of Social Welfare	Central government	National	School enrollment and attendance
26. Mongolia	50	Child Money Program	Ministry of Social Welfare and Labor	Asian Development Bank	National	School enrollment
	51	Child Money Program	Ministry of Social Welfare and Labor	Asian Development Bank	National	School enrollment
27. Pakistan	52	Participation in Education through Innovative Scheme for the Excluded Vulnerable	National Education Foundation	Japan Social Development Fund	National	School attendance
	53	Punjab Female School Stipend Program	Provincial Education Department	World Bank	State	School attendance
	54	Child Support Program	Ministry of Social Welfare and Special Education	Central government	National	School attendance and passing final exam
28. Philippines	55	Pantawid Pamilyang Pilipino Program (innitially AHON)	Department of Social Welfare and Development	Central government and World Bank	National	School attendance

(continued)

Table 2.2 (continued)

Region	Country		Program	Responsible government institution	Funding sources	Scope	Education-related condition
	29. Turkey	56	Social Risk Mitigation Project	General Directorate of Social Assistance and Solidarity	World Bank	National	School attendance
Middle East	30. Yemen	57	Basic Education Development Project	Ministry of Education	Central government and World Bank	National	School attendance and grade promotion
Africa	31. Burkina Faso	58	Nahouri Cash Transfers Pilot Project	National Council against HIV/AIDS and STDs	Central government and World Bank	Regional	School attendance
	32. Congo	59	LISUNGI Safety Nets Project	Ministry of Social Affairs	Central Government, World Bank, Unicef, and French Cooperation Agency	National	School attendance
	33. Egypt	60	Ain el-Sira Project (Cairo)	Ministry of Social Solidarity	Central government	Municipal	School attendance
		61	Takaful	Ministry of Social Solidarity	Central government and World Bank	Regional	School attendance
	34. Ghana	62	Livelihood Empowerment against Poverty	Ministry of Manpower, Youth and Employment	Central Government, World Bank, Unicef, DFID	National	School attendance
	35. Guinea	63	Cash Transfer for Health, Nutrition and Education	Central Government	Central government and World Bank	National	School attendance

(continued)

Table 2.2 (continued)

Region Country		Program	Responsible government institution	Funding sources	Scope	Education-related condition
36. Kenya	64	Cash Transfers for Orphans and Vulnerable Children	Ministry of Home Affairs	Central Government, World Bank, Unicef, DFID, and SIDA	National	School attendance
37. Madagascar	65	Le Transfert Monétaire Conditionnel	Ministry of Education	Central government	Regional	School attendance
38. Morocco	66	Morocco's Cash Transfer for Children (Tayssir Program)	Ministry of Education	Central government and World Bank	National	School attendance
	67	Direct Assistance to Widows in a Precarious Situation with Dependent Children	Ministry of Solidarity, Family, Women and Social Development; Ministry of Interior	Central government	National	School attendance
39. Mozambique	68	Bolsa Escola	Ministry of Education	Brazil/Missao Crianca	District (Maputo)	School attendance
40. Namibia	69	Child Maintenance Grant	Ministry of Gender Equality and Child Welfare	Central government	National	School attendance
41. Nigeria	70	In Care of the Poor	National Agency for the Poverty Eradication Program, Office of the Senior Assistant to the President	Central government	National	School attendance

(continued)

Table 2.2 (continued)

Region	Country		Program	Responsible government institution	Funding sources	Scope	Education-related condition
	42. Senegal	71	Conditional Cash Transfer for Orphans and Vulnerable Children	National HIV/AIDS Council	Central government	National	School attendance
		72	*Programme National de Bourses de Sécurité Familiale*	General Delegation for Social Protection and National Solidarity	Central government	National	School enrollment
	43. South Africa	73	CCT to Support Vulnerable Children in the Context of HIV/AIDS and Poverty	Ministry of Social Development	South African Government	National	School attendance
	44. Tanzania	74	Community-based Conditional Cash Transfer	Central Government	Central Government, World Bank, Unicef, DFID, USAID and WFP	National	School attendance
	45. Tunisia	75	Programme National d'Aide aux Familles Nécessiteuses	Ministry of Social Affairs	Central government, World Bank and Japan Social Development Fund	National	School enrollment

bold move beyond the attempt to improve the access to education, with only a few cases where graduation and performance have been addressed.

In fact, the three cases explored in this book are good examples of different arrangements of education-related conditions and how the educational sector got involved and worked with these programs. A typical case will be presented—*Bolsa Familia*—as well as two other cases in which there was real experimentation with educational conditions. One important aspect for analysis here is the role education institutions and actors have played in these programs and what impact has been produced on the education policy.

But before we move to exploring the programs in detail, we should try to understand better how CCTs became global in the first place. The following section presents an exploration of the various possibilities of scholarly approaches to policy diffusion, especially those that may help us make sense of the global trajectory of the CCT policy model.

2.1   ALTERNATIVE THEORIES TO EXPLAIN CCT'S WORLDWIDE DIFFUSION

Following a growing political and academic interest in the issues posed by globalization, scholars across several disciplines have addressed examples of policy transfer or the international diffusion of norms and policies (Jules and Morais de Sa e Silva 2008). The identification that local experiences have been used as models—or at least as inspiration—for the design of similar policies in other geopolitical contexts has sparked the interest of sociologists, political scientists, and education scholars. In those different fields, scholars have used their disciplinary backgrounds to devise explanations and descriptions of why and how policy diffusion occurs. In the following sections, I present a snapshot of those alternative explanations and later seek to present my own take on what may be the story behind the vast international diffusion of CCTs.

2.1.1   *Policy Transfer and Diffusion*

Dolowitz and Marsh (2000, 3) define policy transfer as "a process in which knowledge about policies, administrative arrangements, institutions and ideas in one political setting (past or present) is used in the development of policies, administrative arrangements, institutions and ideas in another political setting." Since that seminal article, numerous other publications have tried to describe, characterize, classify, and explain the policy transfer phenomenon.

Stone (2012) makes an extensive review of over 800 journal articles dedicated to the topic, revealing that several terms are used to name processes of these kinds, with slight conceptual differences: "diffusion," "transfer," "convergence," and "translation." According to Stone, the policy transfer literature is especially interested in the motivations and decision-making rationale of agents involved in policy transfer. The convergence literature, in turn, rather emphasizes the role of structures, institutions, and other globalization processes as the drivers of global policy isomorphism. Finally, scholars who have worked with the idea of translation are focused on studying the modifications, mutations, and adaptations that these policies undergo when exported/imported.

A part of the policy transfer literature was dedicated to explaining the underlying reasons for diffusion/transfer. According to Weyland (2006), for instance, a policy model diffuses because decision-makers operate under conditions of limited rationality. Since they do not have access to information about every existing policy, it is more immediate and "rational" to adopt "cognitive shortcuts" and emulate foreign models that have been successful in their places of origin, even if they are not the most appropriate for their contexts.

Reaching out to theoretical frameworks and concepts of cognitive psychology, Weyland (2006) explains that the adoption of foreign models takes place due to the "heuristics of availability," the "heuristics of representativeness," and the "heuristics of anchoring." In the first case, decision-makers adopt bold and accessible models, such as those that are world renowned and promoted by international organizations. Besides, decision-makers project themselves in the foreign experience and envision that it is possible and desirable to reach the same results that have been achieved elsewhere. Finally, the heuristics of anchoring limits some later adaptations of foreign models, as those who adopted them tend to get attached to the original version.

In fact, Sugiyama (2008) identifies that Weyland's view belongs to one among three streams of interpretations of the motivations behind policy transfer. According to her, there is the rational-choice political perspective, which looks into the expected political gains that could arise from emulating someone's policy model. Weyland does not directly follow that perspective, but is in fact trying to dialogue with it by proposing a bounded-rationality alternative. Second, there is the ideology-inspired perspective, according to which decisions follow principled ideas, even though this may come at a political cost. Finally, there is the community perspective, for which relations, networks, and socialization processes matter the most in decision-making processes. For Sugiyama, these different perspectives are directly linked to the disciplinary field in which they emerged and to the methods that have been used in research.

Evans (2004) identifies a set of variables that are likely to be barriers to policy transfer: cognitive barriers, environmental barriers, and the domestic and international public opinion. However, among these factors there are no variables related to the characteristics of the public policy being transferred. In fact, most of the policy transfer literature does not address the content of the policy models that are subject to transfer. Howlett and Rayner (2008, 386, cited by Stone 2012, 487) present their critique to that, stating that "what is being transferred sometimes gets lost in the midst of the concern about how transfer happens."

Dolowitz and Marsh (2000) point out that one of the exceptions in this regard is the work of Richard Rose (1993) on lesson learning. According to Rose, the more complex is a program, the smaller is its chance to get transferred to another jurisdiction. He presents seven hypotheses, one of which is as follows: "the simpler is the structure of cause and effect of a program, the more fungible it will be" (1993, 132).

In fact, the CCT model is of relative simplicity. It directly connects government funds with poor families and demands that they access education and health services without having to deal with education and health providers. As the later chapters will discuss, CCTs have impacted education without producing any real education reforms. In order to operate, the program model only demands some targeting strategy in order to define the beneficiary population, some method of cash delivery (i.e., through bank cards or in-person delivery), and some method of conditionality verification. Anything other than that would be a plus derived from some other policy goal, such as allowing for experimentation, for instance.

2.1.2   Theories of Comparative and International Education

In education, the concept of "educational transfer" (Beech 2012) or "policy borrowing and lending" (Steiner-Khamsi 2004; Steiner-Khamsi and Stolpe 2006) has been a common object of study. The concept encompasses processes of transposition of educational models created in one country to another country, where it is hoped it will lead to similar results. According to Beech (2012), the practice of educational transfer is almost as old as the research efforts of the first comparativists in education, who dedicated themselves to not only analyzing the similarities and differences between national educational systems, but were fundamentally involved in identifying positive experiences that could be used to generate successful reforms in other national contexts.

In the framework of the debate between different theories of globalization in education, the borrowing and lending literature has contributed by telling the stories underlying the idea behind the lessons learned from abroad, for the purpose of improving educational policies at home. Its arguments are different and in dialogue with the World Culture Theory in education and with the anthropological perspective on globalization in education (Steiner-Khamsi and Stolpe 2006).

Some of the works within the borrowing and lending literature are based on the idea of externalization (Schriewer and Martinez 2004), according to which policymakers reach out to foreign models in order to justify reform processes that have been domestically developed. Hence, foreign reform models are a certification strategy for reform proposals that meet great opposition at home and are therefore in need of greater legitimacy. Such a certification "label" is achieved when reference is made to an international best practice. Hence, for borrowing and lending scholars, globalization in education is only imagined and borrowing happens only at the discursive level, and not actually at the policy implementation level.

Besides what the authors call the "politics of borrowing and lending" (Steiner-Khamsi 2004), which consists of borrowing as a political certification strategy, there is also the economics of borrowing and lending. In this case, the import of foreign policy models is also related to the possibility of accessing aid and loans from traditional donors and international development banks.

By pointing out the political and economic factors that may motivate policy transfer, borrowing and lending scholars deconstruct some of the arguments presented by neoinstitutionalists in education, according to whom globalization has been naturally turning all education policies alike. Borrowing and lending scholars rather emphasize the agency and motives behind such processes of apparent "policy isomorphism."

In a more recent work, Steiner-Khamsi (2014) differentiates between normative and analytical studies of education policy diffusion, indicating that one of the questions raised in analytical studies is "in what conditions the dissemination of a practice is more likely to happen" (p. 154).

2.1.3   Theories of Norm Diffusion

In the field of international relations, an important group of scholars has analyzed the emergence and implementation of international human rights norms (Risse et al. 1999, 2013; Simons 2009). The literature on the norm life cycle particularly presents a theoretical framework that attempts to explain the impact of human rights norms in influencing the behavior of states. Such literature connects, for instance, with political science studies interested in the international diffusion process of principled ideas.

This is where the intersection lies between policy transfer studies and theories of the norm life cycle. Human rights norms and foreign policy models can influence the decisions and policies adopted by domestic agents. They are both external factors, of voluntary adoption, and are not self-applicable. Hence, they depend on the interest and decision of local mandataries to be internalized. Moreover, human rights policies, just like human rights norms, carry moral principles and meaning.

The norm life cycle literature belongs to the field of constructivist theories in international relations, according to which the interests of actors are not given and can be altered through time. If there is persuasion, the decision-makers may be convinced of the importance of adhering to and complying with human rights treaties.

Naturally, case studies analyzed herein are not about the signature and ratification of treaties. Nonetheless, one could argue that, when involved in policy transfer processes, decision-makers adhere to foreign models. As in the case of human rights norms, this kind of adoption is not mandatory. One could think of persuasion processes though, where local and foreign actors—such as international organizations—convince authorities and managers that there are advantages and value in the external model, to the point that they consider it to be in their interest to engage in policy transfer.

Finally, just as it is expected that human rights norms will produce domestic change, leading states to cease violations, it is expected that the adoption of a new and supposedly positive policy model will produce a positive change in adopting countries, especially developing ones.

Theories of international relations are more than often attempts to explain the decisions made by states in the international arena and, as in other theories, the idea of rationality is used to explain decision patterns. In this framework, the idea of interests is a central construct, based upon which one could explain options and choices. However, depending on the adopted theoretical stance, once could understand interests as something fixed and given, or as a flexible variable that could be redefined on the basis of social interaction processes. "Social constructivists emphasize that ideas and communicative processes define in the first place which material factors are perceived as relevant and how they influence understandings of interest, preference, and political decisions" (Risse et al. 1999, p. 7). Along these lines, Finnemore (1996, p. 2) argues that "interests are not just 'out there' waiting to be discovered; they are constructed through social interaction." This debate is central for those dedicated to researching development cooperation, where material factors tend to receive greater attention, whereas the role of ideas and values remains understudied. The constructivist perspective, beyond recognizing the role of interests, does so in a sophisticated way, recognizing the dynamism that undercuts interests through socialization processes.

The spiral model proposed by Risse et al. (1999, 2013) involves the idea that the impact of international human rights norms on the behavior of states is linked to the socialization processes in which those states participate. These processes are: "processes of instrumental adaptation and strategic bargaining; processes of moral consciousness-raising, argumentation, dialogue, and persuasion; processes of institutionalization and habitualization" (Risse and Sikkink 1999, p. 5).

In an attempt to extend that model to policy transfer processes, one could similarly think of the adoption of foreign models as part of socialization processes in which states want to participate in the club of nations that have adopted a certain kind of policy model, especially if it has been cheered as a "best practice." Decision-makers, besides their material and instrumental motives, can be convinced that such a model is one that best responds to their interests. Here, the role of international organizations, as it has been pointed out earlier in this chapter, may be particularly important for the creation of this socialization effect. As they promote conferences, workshops, and other experience-sharing events among government representatives, they become increasingly familiar with the "best practice" of the day.

In this framework, the role of persuasion is of great importance. Risse and Sikkink (1999, p. 14) "claim that the logic of persuasion and of discourse is conceptually different from a logic of information exchange based on fixed preferences, definitions of the situations, and collective identities. Discursive processes are precisely the types of human interaction in which at least one of these properties of actors is being challenged." Hence, although numerous international cooperation initiatives are geared toward the exchange of information about policy experiences, one could argue that these experiences will only be truly incorporated by countries if decision-makers are persuaded that the experiences fulfill their interests.

Last but not least, Simons (2009) theorizes about the internalization of human rights treaties and, in so doing, also identifies that the most important variables are not so much related to external factors, such as the pressure by other states, but rather, they are linked to local agents themselves. In her words, "treaties are causally meaningful to the extent that they empower individuals, groups, or parts of the state with different rights preferences that were not empowered to the same extent in the absence of the treaties" (p. 125). Likewise, one could argue that foreign models will only be internalized if they are thought to be in the interest of local actors.

2.1.4   An Alternative Explanation

I have been arguing elsewhere that policy content or policy features matter for policy diffusion. Irrespective of decision-makers' motivations, the nature and characteristics of a policy are relevant variables in the policy diffusion process. Contrary to what a functionalist approach might pose, this does not have to do with a policy being successful or a "best practice." As Kingdon (1995) suggests, many policy solutions may exist in the "garbage can," but only a few will find a policy window and will be eventually implemented.

In Morais de Sá e Silva (2016), I examine various cases where Brazil deliberately attempted to transfer its human rights policies by means of cooperation projects established with other countries from the South. By contrasting these cases, it became clear that policies that involved social participation and, therefore, some kind of power-sharing, did not get successfully transferred as much as policies that involved mechanisms for policy coordination leading to power-gaining. Beyond questions of whether these findings conform to a more rational-choice perspective in terms of motivations, the fact is that policy features did matter.

Similarly, it could be argued that CCT's characteristics have had a bearing on their exponential and systematic diffusion worldwide. Again, one could point out their positive evaluation results in some countries. That could certainly be an "attraction factor," but I would argue that this is only part of the story. Positive results may spark interest, but may not be enough to sustain the interest. Also, there is a long way for the actual adoption and implementation of a new policy, even if the model has been "copied" from elsewhere and the package seems ready for use.

Steiner-Khamsi (2004) argues that there is no real policy adoption and that there is only "phony borrowing" (Phillips 2004, p. 57). According to her, policymakers pretend they are importing foreign models, when they are actually just making reference to the model in order to build legitimacy around ideas that have been grown nationally. According to her, what happens in fact is "brand name piracy" rather than real policy borrowing.

However, by looking at the dozens of CCTs that have been implemented in the developing world, it is hard to deny that there is actual diffusion and transfer. What can be questioned, though, is that it seems that what has been traveling internationally is not so much a complete policy model. What has been traveling is actually the idea of the direct transfers of cash from the government to citizens, in a way that their families can be less poor, today and tomorrow. Any definition or specification beyond that basic idea has been amenable to adjustment and change by national and local governments, as the three cases to be presented in this book will later show. And I would argue that it is exactly because this basic idea may fit into different ideologies and may be put in practice in a multitude of ways, that it has been so easily and quickly incorporated. Governments have had the liberty to design and implement CCTs as they wish and by deploying the most diverse kinds of discourses around them. Like clay, the CCT idea is moldable and foldable to any ideological, political, cultural, and social background. Like LEGO pieces, it can be assembled small or tall, thin or fat, cheap or expensive, very simple, or really complex. Its openness attracted the attention not only of policymakers, but also of researchers, who were eager to experiment with them.

So what does it mean to say that policy content matters for policy diffusion in the case of CCTs? First, it means that the CCT model, even if it is more of an idea, is not prescriptive or dependent in terms of program size, mode of implementation, selection of beneficiaries, and so on. Governments can design CCTs in a variety of ways and they will still be considered CCTs, drawing the same interest from the international and academic communities. Second, it is that openness in terms of design that makes them travel easily, because they travel light. To some extent, this is a real lesson on initiatives around policy innovation and their diffusion across different contexts.

Using the argument that was put forward in Morais de Sá e Silva (2016), certain program features speak better about the interests of local policymakers than others. Some features may be actually contrary to those interests, making it less likely that a certain policy model will be transferred. In the case of CCTs, they were simultaneously popular worldwide, brought the possibility of foreign funding, and could be molded into a multitude of different discourses and modes of implementation, provided that some fundamental ideas were kept.

In fact, the CCT brand came in only after years of existence of some programs that had already carried those basic features, but were not explicitly linked to poverty reduction. For instance, Bangladesh and India have had, since the 1990s, a number of cash transfer schemes targeted at girls, with the aim of reducing the "missing women" phenomenon and increasing girls' education. Very little has been said about those South Asian experiences though, which were deeply related to education.

Anyhow, although policy content matters, one cannot leave aside the important role of policy actors. In this case, it is unquestionable that international organizations, especially the World Bank, have been important policy entrepreneurs in making the CCT model cross national borders. Just as norm entrepreneurs are important in the theory of the norm life cycle, policy entrepreneurs with a global reach are very important for a policy model—or policy idea, if you wish—to become truly global. In this case, international organizations, banks, and bilateral donors were important not only for the funding and loans they provided, but also for the community of practice they stimulated. Three international conferences were organized by the World Bank and its national partners: the first in Mexico in 2002, the second in Brazil in 2004, and the third in Mexico in 2006. The conferences gathered specialists and program managers from across the globe with the aim to:

(...) share experience and knowledge among and between countries with extensive experience in CCT and newcomers on what works and what does not work both from a policy and operational perspectives. About 350 people from around the world representing countries implementing or interested in CCT and their counterparts from the World Bank, donor agencies and relevant NGO are attending the conference. (World Bank 2006)

In addition to the conferences, the bank was also responsible for commissioning a number of studies and evaluations of CCTs, of which the Fiszbein and Schady 2009 book—Conditional Cash Transfers: Reducing present and future poverty—is the best example. The book represents a major effort toward mapping out various CCT programs and the corresponding studies that have been developed around them.

Other smaller, but relevant, organizations have also played the role of connecting CCT experiences to policymakers. That is the case of the International Policy Center for Economic Growth (IPC-IG), originally created as the International Poverty Center and linked to the United Nations Development Program (UNDP). Since its creation, the IPC-IG has directed part of its resources toward studying poverty reduction programs, especially CCTs, and sharing the "lessons learned" among practitioners. Its mission is "to promote policy dialogue and facilitate learning between developing countries around innovative social policies for inclusive growth" (IPC-IG 2016).

Finally, although CCTs may be more of an idea, rather than a clearly specified policy model, they are fundamentally attached to the agenda that brought them to life: poverty reduction. They are not fundamentally educational programs, as it will be later discussed. They are not married to political thought on the Right or Left, as we will also discuss. However, they can only survive if the reduction of poverty is on the agenda and if governments and international organizations are willing to spend resources on them. As the following chapters will show, CCTs have survived as long as there was money to maintain them. However, if the priority is no longer fighting poverty and becomes something else (fiscal adjustment, sustainable development, and employment generation), then they might be doomed and the CCT slope may turn downward.

The following chapter will present a selection of theoretical frameworks that can help us better understand the political sustainability of CCT programs, as well as whether and how they have impacted education policies and reforms. Mostly coming from the policy sciences, these frameworks will help us to explore and analyze real CCT cases to be presented in Part II of this book.

NOTE

1. The appraisal of programs has been done according to the following criteria: (i) only cash-based programs were considered, therefore excluding school-feeding programs or those based on school fee waivers; (ii) unconditional programs were not considered; (iii) education-related conditions should be among the pre-established conditionalities; consequently, programs with health-related conditions only or conditions of other sorts were not included.

REFERENCES

Baker, D., & LeTendre, G. (2005). *National differences, global similarities: World culture and the future of schooling.* Stanford: Stanford University Press.

Beech, J. (2012). Quem está passeando pelo jardim global? Agências educacionais e transferência educacional. In R. Cowen, A. Kasamias, & E. Ulterhalter (Orgs.). *Educação comparada: Panorama internacional e perspectivas* (pp. 396–416). Brasília: UNESCO, CAPES.

Dolowitz, D., & Marsh, D. (2000). Learning from abroad: The role of policy transfer in contemporary policy-making. *Governance, 13,* 5–24.

Evans, M. (2004). *Policy transfer in global perspective.* Burlington: Ashgate.

Finnemore, M. (1996). *National Interests In International Society.* New York: Cornell University Press.

Fiszbein, A., & Schady, R. (2009). *Conditional cash transfers: Reducing present and future poverty.* Washington, DC: World Bank.

Hess, F. (1999). *Spinning wheels: The politics of urban school reform.* Washington, DC: Brookings Institution Press.

Howlett, M., & Rayner, J. (2008). Third generation policy diffusion studies and the analysis of policy mixes: Two steps forward and one step back? *Journal of Comparative Policy Analysis, 10*(4), 385–402.

IPC-IG. (2016). *About IPC-IG.* Retrieved October 19, 2016, from http://www.ipc-undp.org/about-us.

Jules, T., & Morais de Sa e Silva, M. (2008). How different disciplines have approached South-South Cooperation and transfer. *Society for International Education Journal, 5*(1), 45–64.

Kingdon, J. (1995). *Agendas, alternatives, and public policies.* New York: Longman.

Morais de Sa e Silva, M. (2010). *Conditional cash transfers and education: United in theory, divorced in policy.* Unpublished doctoral dissertation, Columbia University, New York.

Morais de Sá e Silva, M. (2016). *Barriers and enablers to the sharing of human rights policies through South-South Cooperation.* Buenos Aires: CLACSO

Phillips, D. (2004). Toward a theory of policy attraction in education. In G. Steiner-Khamsi (Ed.), *The global politics of educational borrowing and lending* (pp. 54–67). New York: Teachers College Press.

Risse, T., Ropp, S., & Sikkink, K. (1999). The power of human rights: international norms and domestic change. New York, UK: Cambridge University Press.

Risse, T., Ropp, S., & Sikkink, K. (2013). The persistent power of human rights: From commitment to compliance. Cambridge: Cambridge University Press.

Risse, T., & Sikkink, K. (1999). The socialization of international human rights norms into domestic practices: Introduction. In T. Risse, S. Ropp, & K. Sikkink (Eds.), *The power of human rights: International norms and domestic change*. New York, Uk: Cambridge University Press.

Rose, R. (1993). Lesson Drawing in Public Policy: A guide to learning lessons across time and space. Chatam House: New Jersey.

Schriewer, J., & Martinez, C. (2004). Constructions of internationality in education. In G. Steiner-Khamsi (Ed.), *The Global Politics of Educational Borrowing and Lending*. New York: Teachers College Press.

Simons, B. (2009). Mobilizing for Human rights: International law in domestic politics. Cambridge, New York: Cambridge University Press.

Steiner-Khamsi, G. (2004). *The politics of educational borrowing and lending*. New York: Teachers College Press.

Steiner-Khamsi, G. (2014). Cross-national policy borrowing: Understanding reception and translation. *Asia Pacific Journal of Education, 34*(2), 153–167.

Steiner-Khamsi, G., & Stolpe, I. (2006). *Educational import: Local encounters with global forces in Mongolia*. Nova Iorque: Palgrave Macmillan.

Stone, D. (2012). Transfer and translation of policy. *Policy Studies, 33*(6), 483–499.

Sugiyama, N. B. (2008). Ideology and networks: The politics of social policy diffusion in Brazil. *Latin American Research Review, 43*(3), 82–108, 285.

Weyland, K. (2006). *Bounded rationality and policy reform: Social sector reform in Latin America*. Princeton: Princeton University Press.

World Bank. (2006). *World Bank and the Government of Turkey Organize 3rd International Conference on Conditional Cash Transfers*. Retrieved October 19, 2016, from http://www.worldbank.org/en/news/press-release/2006/06/26/world-bank-and-the-government-of-turkey-organize-3rd-international-conference-on-conditional-cash-transfers.

CHAPTER 3

Framing the Study of CCT Cases

3.1 THEORETICAL FRAMEWORK

Scholarly work on public policies or what some have called the "policy sciences" (Stone 2002) have departed from a range of different assumptions in striving to better understand policy-related matters. Different positions as per the role of politics, institutions, rationality, and other variables in the world of policies have culminated in different theoretical streams. Many attempts have been made at arriving at a typology of theoretical perspectives on public policies. For instance, Kraft and Furlong (2007) differentiate between elite theory, group theory, institutional theory, rational choice theory, and political systems theory. Others see the main cleavage lying between the works of pluralists and those who conceptualize policymaking as being first and foremost conflict-laden (Baumgartner and Jones 1993). Henig (2008), in turn, makes a typology of the different views regarding the use of scientific evidence in policymaking. He sees the most contrasting difference between those who adopt a political perspective according to which research is a political tool and those with a more administrative perspective, which preaches that it is possible to "speak truth to power" (p. 18).

"Best practices" such as conditional cash transfers (CCTs) are favored by the "administrative perspective" of public policy, which promotes the notion of policymaking as an objective and technical process in which expertise is put at the service of finding remedies for societal malfunctions. That perspective has become mainstream in the current era of the

© The Author(s) 2017

M. Morais de Sá e Silva, *Poverty Reduction, Education, and the Global Diffusion of Conditional Cash Transfers*, DOI 10.1007/978-3-319-53094-9_3

"post-bureaucratic state" (Pons and van Zanten 2007; Steiner-Khamsi 2009), which emphasizes scientifically based research and the search for the "killer study" (Hess and Henig 2008). The prevailing expectations are that research findings will define which policies work best, those being called "best practices".

However, this study is not informed by mainstream administrative lenses. It rather adopts a "political perspective" of public policies, one that is interested in the embedded politics of policymaking processes and their "policy paradoxes" (Stone 2002). This political look at a cherished policy solution can provide greater understanding of what that policy means.

To some extent, this research is also based on the premises of conflict theories, signaling to the unequal power resources of different groups and the conflictive nature of politics. The adoption of a conflict theory perspective is reflected in the relevance given by this study to issues of political support to the public policy in question.

This study also belongs to current debates in the field of public management, which has been dominated by the "New Public Management" proposal in the framework of the idea of a "post-bureaucratic State" (Pons and van Zanten 2007; Steiner-Khamsi 2009). The literature on new public management emerged as a consequence of frustrations with the welfare state and the rigid bureaucratic model that dominated it. Having first emerged in the United Kingdom and in the United States, advocates of a new public management have argued that public institutions and civil servants need to be assigned greater autonomy and flexibility and should be assessed in terms of the results they deliver, rather than of the rules they comply with. In the framework of these debates, it has also been pointed out that the complex policy problems of the twenty-first century demand efforts and solutions that depend on a wide array of actors, rather than on single institutions (Martins 2009). Issues such as climate change, food security, and poverty reduction are just a few examples of these multidimensional and multisector problems. Consequently, adequate coordination and integration between different sectors and institutions became a *sine qua non* condition for the effective performance of public policies. In the case of CCTs, their design expresses in itself the recognition that poverty is a multidimensional problem (Levy 2006). However, the fact that CCTs overcame traditional poverty programs by incorporating educational and health measures does not mean that the three sectors—social work, education, and health—are in practice working closely together in the planning and implementation of the programs.

Going hand-in-hand with the new public management debate is the idea of a "network state" operating in a "network society" (Castells 1998). On the one hand, the network state operates as a network itself, with its various bodies being horizontally interlinked and sharing tasks and responsibilities. On the other hand, the network state is a part of a broader network that is also comprised of private and nongovernmental actors, both at the national and transnational levels. CCTs are a good example of a policy that demands intergovernmental coordination of the kind that would be present in an ideal network state. Additionally, such a multitude of actors is present at the international level and there is much interaction between governments implementing CCTs, international organizations, bilateral aid agencies, think tanks, and private foundations, to mention just a few.

According to Saravia (2007), public policy analyses may have at least one or a combination of the following foci:

1. Political content: involves analyzing how the policy was politically adopted and developed;
2. Policy process: looks at some or all phases of the policy cycle;
3. Policy products: entails looking, among other things, at costs and benefits;
4. Policy analysis geared toward providing inputs to decision-making and policymaking;
5. Policy process analysis with the goal of helping to perfect the policymaking process;
6. Policy analysis with the goal of influencing the adoption of a specific alternative or perspective.

Bearing that in mind, this study is partially focused on the policy process and partially on the political content of CCT adoption, implementation, and maintenance in some countries. Within policy studies, this research belongs to the theories of policy process, specifically those that have dedicated efforts to studying policy change and continuity. In education, this research relates to scholarly works on urban education that are interested in better understanding how education reforms are sustained.

Among the various theories of the policy process, two of them stand out as the most useful for this research: the "advocacy coalition framework" (Sabatier and Jenkins-Smith 1993, 1999; Sabatier 1999), and the "punctuated-equilibrium theory"[1] (Baumgartner and Jones 1993, 2002, 2005).

As explained below, the advocacy coalition framework, different from other frameworks, explicitly assigns importance to the relationship between different policy subsystems, such as education and social development in the case of CCTs.

The punctuated-equilibrium theory looks into stability and change in the policy process and argues that the continuity of a policy is assured by a policy monopoly. In education, the "civic capacity scholarship" has used the concept of civic capacity to address the survival of an education policy over time. What triggered the development of the civic capacity framework was the observed lack of continuity in education policies. For such scholars, if there is bottom-up, broad-based support to a policy, it is then able to survive for longer periods.

The following subsections review the literature from each of the bodies of theoretical work: the advocacy coalition framework, punctuated-equilibrium theory, and the civic capacity scholarship. Each subsection presents the conceptual tools and explanatory models that each framework offers to this study. These frameworks will be used in Chaps. 4, 5, and 6 to look into whether and how case-CCTs have impacted education policy and reform, as well as how politically sustainable these programs are in their corresponding contexts.

3.1.1   Advocacy Coalition Framework

The advocacy coalition framework (ACF) is an explanatory model according to which policy change is a function of three processes: (1) competing coalitions that seek to gain control over policies in a given subsystem; (2) external changes in "socioeconomic conditions, system-wide governing coalitions and output from other subsystems that provide opportunities and obstacles to the competing coalitions" (Sabatier and Jenkins-Smith 1993, p. 5); and (3) changes in the social structure or in constitutional rules. Some of these processes, when combined, can then lead to policy change.

Specifically, the framework predicts that "changes in core elements of public policies require the replacement of one dominant coalition by another, and this transition is hypothesized to result primarily from changes external to the subsystem" (pp. 5–6). Of central relevance to this work is the importance that the ACF assigns to external change, especially in terms of change in other subsystems. In this regard, considering that CCTs are novel poverty-reduction programs that have altered the subsystem of social welfare policies in various countries, of interest here is whether they have induced change in the education subsystem, either after being integrated or not into education. In order to accomplish that, it would be necessary to "affect the constraints and opportunities of subsystem actors" (Sabatier and Jenkins-Smith 1999, p. 120), and allow for the replacement of the coalition that dominates education policies at the federal, state, or city level. The importance of external factors for policy change in a given subsystem is attributed to the fact that external change may favor the policy arguments and beliefs of the "opposition" coalition to the detriment of those of the "dominant" coalition.

A differential aspect of the ACF and one that has important implications for research is that policy actors or policy elites are not clustered according to their position or institutional affiliation. Rather, they are understood as members of different advocacy coalitions. According to Sabatier and Jenkins-Smith (1999), advocacy coalitions are "composed of people from various governmental and private organizations that both (1) share a set of normative and causal beliefs and (2) engage in a nontrivial degree of coordinated activity over time" (p. 120). The bonding element of a coalition is their "belief system," which is comprised by "value priorities, perceptions about causal relationships, perceptions of world states (including the magnitude of the problem), and perceptions of the efficacy of policy instruments" (pp. 119–120). Thus, a first step in the use of the advocacy coalition framework involves mapping out the competing belief systems, what actors subscribe to each of them, and what coalitions form around them and compete to gain control over the policy subsystem. It should be mentioned that the ACF expands the definition of policy actors beyond government officials to also include researchers, journalists, and any other nontraditional actors that actively participate in an advocacy coalition.

Belief systems, which are the "soul" of each advocacy coalition, have three main components that maintain a hierarchical relationship. First and at the broadest level, belief systems have a deep core that defines what the coalition's main values are (i.e., viewing education as valuable in itself or as an instrument to achieving economic development). Then, policy core beliefs represent policy priorities, such as investing in primary education or in higher education. Finally, there are secondary aspects that are specific and concrete policy preferences, which are reasonable in the framework of the deep core and the policy core beliefs (Sabatier and Jenkins-Smith 1999). Support to the adoption of CCTs, for instance, could be one of the secondary aspects of a coalition's belief system.

3.1.2   Punctuated-Equilibrium Theory

In order to address the issue of policy sustainability, this research will utilize and contrast the punctuated-equilibrium theory and the civic capacity framework. Baumgartner and Jones' punctuated-equilibrium theory (PET) establishes that a shift from a period of policy continuity (or incremental change) to substantial policy change will happen when new principles of policy action become widely accepted (Baumgartner and Jones 1993). On the other hand, lack of substantial policy change is seen as the result of a policy monopoly, which is "a monopoly on political understandings concerning the policy of interest and an institutional arrangement that reinforces that understanding" (Baumgartner and Jones 1993, p. 6).

Policy monopolies are controlled by some groups but are maintained thanks to a positive and well-accepted policy image. The policy image is the "prevalent understanding of the policy" (Baumgartner and Jones 1993, p. 7). If the policy image is able to harness public support (or not to evoke opposition), then policy monopolies may be formed or maintained. According to the ACF terms, one can say that a policy monopoly occurs when a coalition's belief system dominates. Different from the advocacy coalition framework, which gives primary importance to coalitions formed across governmental and nongovernmental institutions, the punctuated-equilibrium theory does assign importance to governmental institutions. Specifically, the theory approaches institutions as policy venues, which are defined as those in society with the authority to make decisions with regard to specific policy issues (Baumgartner and Jones 1993). Additionally, policy venues are centrally important in defining whether a policy image will be supported or rejected. For instance, training programs of only six months may not be accepted by a department of education for the training of its teachers, but may be considered reasonable by a department of labor or a department of finance seeking to reduce costs and achieve quick results. This is what Baumgartner and Jones call the "image-venue interaction" (p. 37).

To some extent, it can be stated that punctuated-equilibrium theory has more of an institutionalist and top-down perspective with regard to the maintenance of public policies. Government institutions are centrally important and other sectors are rather considered as "consumers" of a positive policy image.

3.1.3   Civic Capacity

Despite glimmers of success and incremental signs of progress, the results of this sustained attention have been disappointing. Hot new reforms and celebrated school reformers cycle through urban school systems in quick succession, raising high hopes that are soon deflated. This pattern, variously labeled as "policy churn," "spinning wheels," and "reform du jour" has engendered a deeper sense of fatalism among some and a desperation-driven readiness to adopt radical solutions among others. (Henig and Rich 2004)

The above quote describes the reality of educational reform, especially in the US,[2] where different education policies come and go due to the sense of urgency for improving a sector that has been blamed for putting the "nation at risk" (National Commission on Excellence in Education 1983). In developing countries, the constant turnover of education policies is not less of an issue. It results from a combination of political instability, influence of foreign donors, frequent economic shocks, and the resulting pressure for fiscal reform.

Concerned about the sustainability of education policies and reforms, a group of political science scholars developed a consistent body of research based on the concept of civic capacity. Stone et al. (2001) define civic capacity as "the involvement of various sectors of the community in a problem-solving effort" (p. 20). Civic capacity scholars have been puzzled about why, despite the wide recognition of the dismal performance of inner-city public schools and recurrent attempts to reform them, improvements have been rare, especially on a sustainable basis (Henig et al. 1999; Stone et al. 2001).

According to the civic capacity framework, ephemeral initiatives have been the rule rather than the exception in education policymaking. The main reason lies in the fact that public school reforms in various US cities have lacked civic capacity, that is, they have not secured broad-based support from education coalitions and from different sectors of the community. Consequently, it is easy to start new education policies but difficult to sustain them over time (Henig et al. 1999; Stone et al. 2001).

The concept of civic capacity shares with the advocacy coalition framework the recognition of nongovernmental actors as important players in the policy process. In the words of Stone (2005), "as a concept, civic capacity rests on the assumption that government and civil society are not discrete spheres of activity (…) What we call public policy is in fact the joint product of governmental and non-governmental actors" (p. 209). Hence, an analysis conducted within the civic capacity framework shall assess not only the level of support to a policy within public agencies but also among actors such as scholars and journalists. Teachers are also considered fundamentally important for the buildup of sufficient civic capacity, as they have often presented resistance to attempts to achieve change and reform (Henig et al. 1999).

Although the civic capacity framework acknowledges business leaders as important policy actors, it also warns against some excessive euphoria around public–private partnerships. After conducting empirical research on urban school systems, civic capacity scholars have concluded that the involvement of business in fostering reform has been ephemeral and ad hoc. In some cases, it has rather contributed to creating distrust in the community, which does more harm than good by eroding the basis for the construction of civic capacity (Henig et al. 1999).

At the core of the civic capacity argument are empirical findings pointing out that, in the presence of community involvement and general policy support, public schools are able to thrive (Stone 2005). In contrast, in contexts marked by distrust, lack of civic capacity makes it difficult for policies to last long (Henig et al. 1999).

Finally, it should be acknowledged that the advocacy coalition framework, the punctuated equilibrium theory, and the civic capacity framework have been developed specifically in the US context, and their authors did not aim at making them applicable to all national contexts. Nonetheless, there are no reasons why a researcher should refrain from using them in developing countries that have adopted democratic political systems, even if their democratic institutions are still fragile.

As mentioned earlier, these frameworks share a major concern for political processes, power disputes, and potential conflict. They do not take institutions at face value and accept the possibility of "policy paradoxes" (Stone 2002). Therefore, even in contexts of imperfect democratic institutions, the basic concepts and theories of action proposed by the US-based frameworks should apply.

3.2   Case-Study Research Design

In order to illuminate the link between education policymaking and CCTs, as well as issues related to CCTs' sustainability, the following chapters will present a comparative study that takes into account the diverse designs and contexts of the programs. As pointed out in Chap. 2, 40 countries have had a pilot or full-fledged CCT. The mode of operation of their programs varies in terms of a number of characteristics: conditionalities, educational goal, institution responsible for implementation, scope, source of funding, and others. At the same time, many of them share various program features.

In order to have a better grasp of the paradoxical diversity of this global policy model, Chap. 4 will present the real policy trajectories of three CCT programs. The selection of cases was guided by an interest in better understanding typical cases, since, as indicated earlier, so many programs share basic characteristics such as their scope, source of funding, and education-related conditions. On the other hand, "outliers" are equally interesting, as a few programs appear as stark exceptions for most of the appraised characteristics. In order to address the common and uncommon cases, three programs were selected: *Bolsa Familia* (Brazil), Opportunity NYC (New York City), and *Subsidios Condicionados a la Asistencia Escolar* (Bogota, Colombia). This selection was also based on the fact that the programs are diverse in terms of the education-related conditions to which their cash benefits are tied: *Bolsa Familia* is conditional upon school attendance, the *Subsidios* program has attendance and graduation conditions, and Opportunity NYC makes transfers dependent upon attendance and improved performance on tests.

Bolsa Familia is the typical case in terms of education-related conditions, besides being "the largest CCT program in the developing world" (UNESCO 2008, p. 153). Most CCT programs follow a similar design of only conditioning payments to children's school attendance. Also, in most countries, *Bolsa Familia* is under the auspices of a social welfare government body. In this regard, both Opportunity NYC and the *Subsidios* program in Bogota are more of an exception. The Bogota program is directly managed by the city's Department of Education, and is linked to a higher education scholarship program, which may work as an additional and forward-looking incentive for high-school completion. In turn, Opportunity NYC has other features that make of it an interesting case to look at: (1) the program was fully funded by philanthropies; (2) New York's public school system was under mayoral control; and (3) it was among the first CCTs to be implemented in a developed country.

Interestingly, this characterization of the three programs in terms of being typical or extreme cases is somewhat different if one looks at the question of political sustainability. The Colombian program seemed to have been implemented without much public opposition and parents and students voiced great appreciation for *Subsidios* (Meyer and Morais de Sa e Silva 2008). In contrast, Opportunity NYC's situation was different in that regard, as criticisms were presented from both ends of the political spectrum (Morais de Sa e Silva 2008). Similarly, in Brazil, the situation of *Bolsa Familia* is currently uncertain, as the conservative forces that led the impeachment process of former President Rousseff are openly against the program.

Hence, the three programs seemed to combine both standard CCT characteristics as well as important peculiarities that arose in their particular contexts. The examination of each case in detail is expected to allow for the consideration of important program characteristics within the complete account of how each of them was developed and the role they played in the educational arena. At the same time, it is expected that, through their comparison, the cases can yield complementary evidence, especially since each program is geared toward improving a different variable in terms of educational attainment—attendance, graduation, and performance.

3.2.1   Data Collection Methods

This research made use of qualitative methods for the analysis and comparison of three case studies. Data collection was carried out at three research sites—New York City, Bogotá, and Brasilia from February 2009 to March 2010 and later since January 2016. The data collection methods were similar across the three cases, involving semistructured interviews, collection of policy documents, and appraisal of press materials and institutional websites.

Interviews
The three frames of theory adopted in this research call for the consideration of a broad array of actors as relevant informants. Whereas the punctuated-equilibrium theory assigns primary importance to policymakers in government institutions, the advocacy coalition framework includes scholars and journalists as participants of advocacy coalitions (Sabatier 1999). In addition, representatives of teachers' unions, teachers, and school principals are highlighted by the civic capacity scholarship as potential builders (or destroyers) of civic capacity (Henig et al. 1999; Stone et al. 2001).

Consequently, considering the kinds of informants that are valued by each of these theories, data were collected from the following categories of interviewees: government officials (both from education and social development government bodies), scholars, leaders of teachers' unions, politicians, staff members of international organizations, representatives of private philanthropies, think tank researchers, and journalists.

Within each category of interviewees, individuals were selected if they met one of the following criteria: (1) individual has played a role in a CCT program; (2) individual has played a role in education policymaking; (3) individual is knowledgeable about CCT program; or (4) individual is knowledgeable about education policymaking debates. These criteria were adopted in order to make sure that the interviewees would be either members of an advocacy coalition (in education or social development) or they would be key informants about the adoption and implementation processes of the CCT case in their city/country.

Additionally, in the case of Bogota, interviews were also conducted with teachers, school principals, and other school personnel. One school was randomly selected from each of the seven city neighborhoods where the program operates. Each school made available different representatives to be interviewed and that is why only the principal was interviewed in some of them, while in others it was also possible to interview teachers and other personnel. That also explains why there were 12 interviews for seven different schools. Although it was not possible to compare the three case studies on the basis of school interviews, they were useful in further illuminating the Bogota experience.

A total of 66 semistructured interviews were conducted across the three cases. The sample of interviewees per case was as given in Table 3.1.

Interview protocols were designed according to the core concepts used by each of the adopted theoretical frameworks. Every interviewee, except for teachers, principals, and other school personnel, answered questions that followed a standardized conceptual structure:

1. Background: basic information about interviewee and his current work position.
2. Belief systems.
3. Participation in advocacy coalition.
4. Replacement of advocacy coalition.
5. Policy image.
6. Previous policies.
7. Civic capacity.

Table 3.1 Set of interviewees per case study

	Government officials	Scholars/ Researchers	Teachers' unions	International organizations	Journalists	Private philanthropies	Think tanks	Congressmen	School principal	School teacher	Other school personnel	Total
Opportunity NYC	5[a]	2	1	1	3	1	1	0	0	0	0	14
Subsídios	8[b]	2	2	4	1	2	2	0	6	3	3	33
Bolsa Família	4	5	0	6	0	0	2	2	0	0	0	19
Total	17	9	3	11	4	3	5	2	6	3	3	66

[a]This number also includes program managers outside of government, since parts of the program have been implemented by contractors

[b]Among these are former and current officials of the city's Department of Education, as well as officials of the national Ministry of Education and of the Social Action Agency, which is linked to the President's Office

The structure was set up in order to obtain data that would allow for the understanding of each case study through the lense of the theoretical framework. Questions were constructed in a way that would later help in mapping out existing advocacy coalitions and appraisal of CCT's policy image and civic capacity.

For government officials in education, two additional sections were added to the interview protocols: CCT adoption in education and CCT funding. These additional sections were aimed at obtaining factual data about the operation of the CCT program within the government educational institution. Besides, during each interview new questions were added to obtain further information and to probe given answers.

For the interviews conducted with school principals, teachers, and other personnel, a completely different set of questions was used. The structure of the interview protocols encompassed the following subsections: background, belief systems, CCT beneficiary students, CCT and education policies, and civic capacity. Although this structure has some of the elements listed above for the other categories of interviewees, most of the actual questions were different, as they were adapted to the schools' experiences.

Furthermore, as the interviews were meant to be semistructured, various questions were added according to the peculiarities of each case and to follow-up on answers that provided interesting and intriguing information.

Data Analysis
Interview notes and recordings were analyzed according to a list of subjects and markers of interest. The list mainly comprised of the following elements:

1. Information on CCT's design process.
2. Factual data on how the CCT operates.
3. Viewpoint of the value of education.
4. Viewpoint of the country's/city's main educational problems.
5. Viewpoint of the country's/city's policy priorities in education.
6. Opinion about the CCT.
7. Opinion about education policies in place.
8. How others think of CCT (known supporters and opponents).

Although the interview protocols were similar across different types of interviewees, some did not have information to answer some questions, did not want to respond to them, or gave replies that went far beyond what was asked. Also, as a part of the semistructured interview, new questions were added as a follow-up to previous answers or to take advantage of the interviewee's privileged position to answer certain questions.

Data on topics that were common across all interviews (i.e., respondent's belief system) were coded and contrasted. Factual data that referred to the CCT's history and the educational and political contexts were transcribed and used to build a narrative on each case study.

It is important to mention that this research intended to develop a dialogue both with the CCT community of managers and with the education community of scholars and practitioners. Consequently, the operational details of each of the researched programs were included, so that both the communities could take advantage of the information that would be of interest to them.

Policy Documents and Newspapers
Policy documents were analyzed in order to obtain background information on the CCT program and on the policies for education quality that were implemented since the adoption of the CCT. Specifically, the following documents were searched: official CCT program documents, laws and decrees, education reports, and program evaluations. The adopted procedure for data analysis mainly involved the search for key information on the CCT's development, mode of operation, and evaluation results, as well as on each case's background in terms of education policymaking.

Finally, this research attempted to capture the "policy image" (Baumgartner and Jones 1993) of each CCT case. In order to accomplish that, newspapers published around the world and specifically in the country and city in question were analyzed. The search process was carried out by means of the Dow Jones Factiva database for the three-year period between 01 January 2007 and 31 December 2009. Following the methods adopted by Baumgartner and Jones (1993) in the framework of the punctuated-equilibrium theory, the materials were used to measure the intensity of coverage (level of attention) and tone (nature of attention).

Intensity of coverage was based on three different criteria: (1) articles in all languages and from all countries; (2) articles in all languages published in the country of the CCT in question; and (3) articles in all languages published in the city of the CCT in question (except for *Bolsa Familia*). Among the articles published in all languages in various countries, the search was refined by requesting for only articles that had been indexed under the subject "education." This allowed for the analysis of whether and to what extent the media had considered the CCT an educational program.

In order to capture the nature of attention and some other aspects of the CCT's policy image, the search combined the program's name with another key word. The key words that were common among cases were: controversial/*controvertido/controverso*; critics/*critico*; interesting/*interesante/interessante*; and successful/*exitoso/bemsucedido*.[3] For each program, articles were searched using the key word in English, then in Spanish, then in Portuguese, and finally the number of articles found for each of them were added up. Additionally, key words that were specifically relevant for a specific CCT were also used. In the case of Opportunity NYC, there were searches for articles that featured the program's name as well as Mexico, *Oportunidades*, or experiment/experimental.

Finally, as the World Bank and the Inter-American Development Bank have been major supporters and funders of CCTs in the Americas, their websites were also subject to investigation. Their search engines were used to find out how many webpages and documents the websites had hosted with information on each CCT. The resulting number of entries was used as a proxy measure of each program's international exposure, as well as of its buy-in by those organizations.

Notes

1. The number of articles that were obtained through this search process is not to be understood as an exact measure, since words like "opposition" and "interesting" may be referring to something else rather than the CCT program.
2. Although both theoretical frameworks were developed to address the policy process in the US, some of their concepts are equally useful for policy studies in other democratic countries.
3. If not in most countries.

REFERENCES

Baumgartner, F., & Jones, B. (1993). *Agendas and instability in American politics.* Chicago: University of Chicago Press.

Baumgartner, F., & Jones, B. (2002). *Policy dynamics.* Chicago: University of Chicago Press.

Baumgartner, F., & Jones, B. (2005). *The politics of attention: How government prioritizes problems.* Chicago: University of Chicago Press.

Castells, M. (1998). *Hacia el Estado Red* (Towards the Network State). Unpublished manuscript presented at the International Seminar on Society and State Reform, São Paulo, March 2008, 26–28.

Henig, J. (2008). *Spin cycle. How research is used in policy debates: The case of charter schools.* New York: Russel Sage Foundation.

Henig, J., Hula, R., Orr, M., & Pedescleaux, D. (1999). *The color of school reform: Race, politics, and the challenge of urban education.* Princeton: Princeton University Press.

Henig, J. R., & Rich, W. C. (2004). *Mayors in the middle: Politics, race, and mayoral control of urban schools.* Princeton: Princeton University Press.

Hess, F., & Henig, J. (2008). 'Scientific research' and policymaking: A tool, not a crutch. *Education Week.* Retrieved February 12, 2008, from http://www.edweek.org/login.html?source=http%3A%2F%2Fwww.edweek.org%2Fsearch.html%3Fqs%3DHenig&destination=http%3A%2F%2Fwww.edweek.org%2Few%2Farticles%2F2008%2F02%2F06%2F22hess.h27.html%3Fqs%3DHenig&lev elId=2100&baddebt=false.

Kraft, M., & Furlong, S. (2007). *Public policy: Politics, analysis, and alternatives.* Washington, DC: CQ Press.

Levy, S. (2006). *Progress against poverty: Sustaining Mexico's Progresa-Oportunidades program.* Washington, DC: Brookings Institution Press.

Martins, H. F. (2009). *Gestão Pública Contemporânea* [Contemporary public management]. São Paulo: Editora Thomson-Cengage.

Mayer, P., & Morais de Sa e Silva, M. (2008). *Bogotá equity in education: Conditional subsidies for school attendance and postsecondary study. A qualitative evaluation.* Unpublished manuscript.

Morais de Sa e Silva, M. (2008). New York's brand-new conditional cash transfer programme: What if it succeeds? *International Poverty Centre One Pager, 60.*

National Commission on Excellence in Education. (1983). *A nation at risk.* Retrieved November 5, 2008, from http://www.ed.gov/pubs/NatAtRisk/index.html.

Pons, X., & van Zanten, A. (2007). *Knowledge circulation, regulation and governance.* Literature review (part 6). Louvain: EU Research Project, Knowledge and Policy in Education and Health Sectors. Retrieved from http://www.knowandpol.eu.

Sabatier, P. (1999). The need for better theories. In P. Sabatier (Ed.), *Theories of the policy process* (pp. 3–17). Boulder: Westview Press.

Sabatier, P., & Jenkins-Smith, P. (1993). *Policy change and learning: An advocacy coalition approach.* Boulder: Westview Press.

Sabatier, P., & Jenkins-Smith, P. (1999). The advocacy coalition framework: An assessment. In P. Sabatier (Ed.), *Theories of the policy process* (pp. 117–168). Boulder: Westview Press.

Saravia, E. (2007). Introdução à teoria da Política Pública. In E. Saravia & E. Ferrarezi (Ed.), *Políticas Públicas* (pp. 21–42). Brasilia: ENAP.

Steiner-Khamsi, G. (2009). Knowledge-based regulation and the politics of international comparison. *Nordisk Pedagogik, 28,* 61–71.

Stone, C. (2005). Civic capacity: What, why and from whence. In S. Fuhrman & M. Lazerson (Eds.). *The public schools* (pp. 209–235). Oxford: Oxford University Press.

Stone, C., Henig, J., Jones, B., & Pierannunzi, C. (2001). *Building civic capacity: The politics of reforming urban schools.* Lawrence: University Press of Kansas.

Stone, D. (2002). *Policy paradox: The art of political decision-making.* New York: Norton.

UNESCO. (2008). *EFA Global Monitoring Report. Education for all by 2015. Will we make it?* Oxford: Oxford University Press.

PART II

The Realities of CCTs in the Global North and the Global South

CHAPTER 4

A Conditional Cash Transfer in the Big Apple

For those who thought that conditional cash transfers (CCTs) were exclusive remedies of the developing world, the adoption of Opportunity NYC in 2007 in the heart of the world's financial capitalism came as a surprise. So far, CCTs had been spreading across developing countries, in many cases following the recommendations and funding of international organizations. As poverty reduction tools, they became critical components of the international development agenda. However, since the developed world is "not entitled" to receive international aid or at least the advice of development experts, CCTs had not been considered as a possible solution for tackling poverty in the industrialized countries.

In New York City the adoption of a CCT was, to some extent, a consequence of the deliberations of the Commission for Economic Opportunity (the "Poverty Commission"), which had been formed by Mayor Bloomberg in 2006 to advise him on how to mitigate poverty in the city. In the midst of discussions about possible strategies to face the city's poverty problems, some commission members (a scholar and representatives of the Rockefeller Foundation) suggested the adoption of a conditional cash transfer program (UN Webcast Archives 2007). These commissioners had got acquainted with the Mexican CCT experience and thought that its innovative model could be adapted to other contexts, including New York City. In June 2006, the Commission organized a conference entitled "*Exploring Strategies to Create Opportunity in New York City.*" The conference included a panel on conditional cash transfers and a World Bank staff member was invited to participate. That

© The Author(s) 2017
M. Morais de Sá e Silva, *Poverty Reduction, Education, and the Global Diffusion of Conditional Cash Transfers*, DOI 10.1007/978-3-319-53094-9_4

marked the Bank's first involvement with the discussions that later led to the creation of Opportunity NYC.

Although the Commission's final report does not explicitly recommend CCTs, the Deputy Mayor took up the idea of looking at these experiences. Efforts were made to obtain further information on Mexico's *Oportunidades*, on the UK's child poverty campaign, and on any similar experiences that might exist in the US. Working on this enterprise were the Rockefeller Foundation; the Center for Economic Opportunity (CEO), which had been created by the Mayor after the Commission's final report; and MDRC,[1] a nonpartisan policy research organization that later was put in charge of Opportunity NYC's impact evaluation.

Initially, program materials, literature on CCTs, and reports provided by the World Bank were shared among partner organizations. Then a two-day workshop was organized in New York in December 2006 with the participation of the top administrators and leading evaluators of Mexico's *Oportunidades*. Furthermore, in April 2007 the Rockefeller Foundation coordinated a study tour to Mexico, where Mayor Bloomberg, Deputy Mayor Linda Gibbs and representatives of partner organizations could get to know the operation of the *Oportunidades* program in greater detail.

The concept of a cash transfer tied to education-seeking behavior resonated with the ideas that Harvard Professor Roland Fryer had been promoting for some time. In 2004, Fryer convinced the NYC School Chancellor to let him expand an experiment that he had been running in Public School 70 in the Bronx, where he introduced small prizes to reward students for achieving better grades. Although data for P.S. 70 had been inconclusive, Chancellor Klein allowed the experiment to be taken to more schools along with the replacement of small prizes by cash incentives (Dubner 2005).

Fryer has based his experiments on the argument that disadvantaged children lack the motivation to perform better in school because they do not have close examples of the future benefits of investing time and effort in education. Consequently, they need a material incentive that will influence their behavior and boost their performance. In an interview to the New York Times Magazine, he said: "I'm troubled by the fact that we're treating kids as inanimate objects. They have behavior, too. They respond to incentives, too" (Dubner 2005). Thus, the idea of adopting a CCT to tackle poverty in the city was coupled with the ideas and practices that Fryer had been promoting in education. As a result,

Opportunity NYC became the first CCT to condition payments on academic achievement, rather than only on enrollment and attendance, as it has been the case of most existing CCTs.

After the first workshop with Mexican officials and the study tour to Mexico, the design process of Opportunity NYC involved a number of meetings that gathered representatives of the core organizations in charge of the program—CEO, MDRC, and Seedco[2]—as well as sponsors and individuals who were invited to help design specific program features. That was the case of the Department of Education (DoE), which was invited to help specify what activities would be rewarded and the corresponding amount of cash incentives.

Initially, Opportunity NYC involved a total budget of US\$ 53.4 million (Center for Economic Opportunity 2009). It was entirely funded by private institutions such as the Rockefeller Foundation, the Starr Foundation, the Robin Hood Foundation, the Open Society Institute, the American International Group, and Mayor Bloomberg himself (Office of the Mayor 2007). According to a CEO representative, the Mayor did not want to put public money into this type of a program until they had some idea of whether it worked or not. The budget was meant to fund a two-year pilot that started in September 2007.

Since the day when the Mayor announced its creation, Opportunity NYC has attracted considerable attention from the media. In most of the press coverage, the program was initially pictured as very controversial, which materialized the administration's initial fears and justified its decision of funding Opportunity NYC with private resources.

4.1   OPPORTUNITY NYC'S FEATURES

The end result of the merge between the Mayor's office's inclination to adopt a CCT and Fryer's efforts to experiment with cash for performance was reflected in the way Opportunity NYC was structured. The bulk of the program, a subprogram called Family Rewards, was managed by City Hall's Center for Economic Opportunity (CEO) and included a plethora of different conditions, which could allow a beneficiary family to receive cash payments every two months. In parallel, the DoE and Roland Fryer's Education Innovation Laboratory managed the Spark subprogram, which targeted only fourth and seventh graders in 58 preselected low-performing schools. There was also a third subprogram called Work Rewards. It was targeted at families that received subsidized housing but did not include any education-related conditions.

4.1.1   Family Rewards

When the media featured Opportunity NYC, articles were actually referring to Family Rewards. The subprogram was under the auspices of CEO, was evaluated by MDRC, and was actually implemented by Seedco with the support of contracted neighborhood partner organizations (NPOs). It was designed as a randomized trial and therefore involved both a treatment and a control group.

The definition of which families should be eligible for the program was first based on geographic targeting. Six low-income neighborhoods in Manhattan, Brooklyn, and the Bronx were chosen.[3] Then, the DoE provided a list of all children who were eligible for free lunch or reduced-price lunch[4] in those communities. With that information in hand, contracted NPOs actively tried to contact the families of those students in order to have them enrolled in the program. Although the original goal was to enroll about 5100 families, only 4778 were eventually enrolled (Miller et al. 2009). Finally, family beneficiaries were chosen through random assignment, resulting in a total pool of program beneficiaries of 2400 families (Center for Economic Opportunity 2009).

Family Rewards had monetary rewards pertaining to three main fields: education, preventive health, and employment and training. According to the Center for Economic Opportunity (2009, pp. 44–45), in the first two years of the program the activities that a family could perform to receive cash payments were as given in Table 4.1.

The inclusion of such an extensive list of "conditionalities" or incentivized activities made the operation and evaluation of Opportunity NYC more complex when compared with other existing CCTs. In most other cases, families are eligible to a lump sum and only fail to receive it if program managers verify that at least one of the conditionalities had not been met. These normally include school enrollment and minimum attendance, immunization of children, health checkups of pregnant women, and attendance of community meetings. In the case of Opportunity NYC, each activity had a monetary value attached to it and payments were only made after compliance had been proven. In other words, whereas most developing countries' CCTs have a rationale of regularly paying a fixed amount of cash if failure to comply with conditions is not verified, Opportunity NYC had an inverse logic of remunerating families per activity performed and demonstrated.

Table 4.1 Opportunity NYC activity list

Field	Activities
Education	- Child attends school 95% of scheduled days - Parent attends Parent–Teacher Conferences - Child gets or has a Public Library Card - Child progresses on standardized tests - Parent discusses annual tests with teachers - High school students only: student passes a Regents Exam; student takes the PSAT; student accumulates 11 credits in school year; student graduates and accumulates 44 credits
Health	- Get/maintain public health insurance or get/maintain private health insurance - Complete a yearly nonemergency medical checkup - Complete physician-advised follow-up - Complete pediatrician-advised early intervention referral and evaluation for a child under 30 months - Complete two dental visits per year for family members 6 years and older - Complete one dental visit per year for family members aged 1–5
Work	- Work at least 30 h per week; - Complete an approved training course

Coupons were also a novelty introduced by Opportunity NYC. Every two months, beneficiary families received a book of coupons for most activities in the above list. Each coupon had identification information for the family and was meant to be signed by the teacher, physician, or employer, depending on the activity being performed. The family should then mail all coupons to Seedco, which would process payments on a bimonthly basis. For most education activities, however, the monitoring of conditionalities was done directly through the matching of administrative data provided by the DoE.

When combined, the two innovations made it harder for families to understand how the program operated and to participate as expected. The fact that beneficiary families were the ones in charge of proving compliance with most conditionalities—as opposed to program administrators getting the data to release payments—made the program more time-consuming for participants. As a result, compliance was relatively low at the beginning of program operation. Throughout its first ten months of implementation, 75% of all participating families received no more than $3600 in total (Center for Economic Opportunity et al. 2008), which is less than 30% of the annual federal poverty line. In the 2010 impact evaluation, program managers acknowledged that Opportunity NYC's high complexity caused operational difficulties, especially leading to a bumpy startup process during the program's first year (Riccio et al. 2010).

The daily operations of Family Rewards were overseen by CEO and carried out by Seedco and (NPOs). Seedco processed all coupons, authorized payments, coordinated marketing activities, and housed the program helpline. Additionally, NPOs supported the program in each targeted neighborhood by providing direct assistance and workshops to families. In the early stage of the program, NPOs were key for the identification of eligible families, their enrollment, and the provision of information on how Family Rewards was supposed to work. Finally, MDRC was the organization in charge of Family Rewards' overall impact evaluation. It was also one of the main players in the program's initial design.

4.1.2   Spark

Spark was a major project by Prof. Roland Fryer and the Education Innovation Laboratory (EdLabs) at Harvard. Fryer has dedicated his career to conducting leading research on racial issues, particularly on the achievement gap between black and white children. EdLabs is based on the idea of evidence-based policymaking and the belief that "we can transform education through the power of the scientific method" (Education Innovation Laboratory 2010). EdLabs' experiments included trials of different strategies that would give underprivileged children a material incentive to improve their performance in school. Besides Spark in New York City, Fryer's team also led two other programs that provided cash for performance: Capital Gains in Washington, DC. and Chicago's Paper Project. In New York, another incentives-for-performance program was tried and evaluated by Fryer's team: the Million Motivation Campaign. Students were given cell phones and were awarded talking minutes according to their academic performance.

Different from Family Rewards, which was targeted at the entire family, Spark targeted individual students. Its focus was exclusively on education. In Family Rewards, children were spread across a number of different schools, which were not involved in any of the program operations. Principals and teachers were rarely aware of which students were program beneficiaries. On the other hand, Spark operated in 58 selected schools and benefited all of their fourth and seventh graders.

Additionally, Spark provided smaller cash incentives, which were paid directly to students, rather than to their parents. Table 4.2 contrasts Family Rewards and Spark in greater detail.

4.2   OPPORTUNITY NYC TIME-EXTENSION

Initially, Opportunity NYC was supposed to be a two-year pilot program. However, in 2009 it was announced that Family Rewards would receive new funding and continue for a third year, although final evaluation results were not available by that time. Interestingly, some initial funders, such as the Robin Hood foundation, were not among the group of sponsors for this third year. According to David Saltzman, the executive director of Robin Hood, the board of the Foundation was still to vote on whether it would continue its support to the program (Bosman 2009). However, since 2007 the Foundation had been critical of the program's design and argued that its continuation should be based on public, not private funds.

The continuation of Family Rewards for a third year involved a tighter budget, which led to the adoption of a "streamlined schedule of incentives" (Miller et al. 2009, p. 12). In other words, there were not enough resources to pay all possible rewards according to the previous list of conditionalities. In order to decide what activities should be cut, CEO, MDRC, and Seedco took into account two factors: operational difficulties and the results of a preliminary impact report. Different from the program design stage, other city agencies such as the DoE were not directly involved in this decision-making process.

The revision of Family Rewards' "incentive menu" involved significant changes in the education conditionalities. For instance, the activity "parental review of tests and discussion with teachers" was eliminated, mostly due to operational difficulties in verifying whether parents had really discussed their children's grades with teachers or just had them sign the coupon. Attendance conditionalities for elementary and middle-school students were also cut. The decision was based on the program's preliminary impact report, according to which Family Rewards had no significant impact on the share of students who attended class for at least 95% of school days. Also due to the report's findings, incentivized activities were concentrated at the high-school level. Consequently, in its third year of operation Family Rewards presented the set of education-related conditions as given in Table 4.3.

Table 4.2   Opportunity NYC Family Rewards and Opportunity NYC Spark

	Family Rewards		Spark
Development and management	CEO, Seedco, MDRC, and selected neighborhood partner organizations		The Education Innovation Laboratory
Beneficiaries	2400 families residing in Central and East Harlem in Manhattan; Brownsville and East New York in Brooklyn; and Morris Heights/ Mount Hope and East Tremont/Belmont in the Bronx		58,000 kids in the first year and 8000 kids in the second year. They are from 58 selected schools and were either in the fourth or seventh grade when they enrolled in the program
Activities and rewards[a]	Condition	Reward	"Students in fourth grade will receive up to $25 for a perfect score on each of 10 interim assessment tests taken throughout the year, up to a total of $250" (Seedco 2008). "Seventh graders can earn up to $50 per test for a maximum payment of $500 per year" (Seedco 2008)
	95% of school attendance per month	$25 per month (elementary and middle school students) $50 per month (high school students)	
	Attending parent–teacher conferences	$25	
	Getting a library card	$50	
	Improvement in scores or proficiency on standardized tests at the elementary and middle school levels	$300 per test (elementary school) $350 per test (middle school)	
	Parental review of the test and discussion with teachers	$25	
	Passing grade on individual Regents exams	$600	
	Student takes the PSAT	$50	
	Student accumulates 11 credits in high school year	$600	
	Student graduates from high school and accumulates 44 credits	$400	

[a]These are the activities and rewards for the first two years of operation of Family Rewards. As explained later in this chapter, budget constraints and research findings led to a revision of the incentive menu used in the third year

4.3 Process and Impact Evaluation

In 2009, Miller, Riccio, and Smith prepared a preliminary impact evaluation report on Family Rewards, with data from the program's first year of implementation. Interestingly, it was solely based on education data. This was because information on compliance with most education activities was readily available through the DoE's databases and did not require the processing of coupons. Using such data, MDRC's team estimated the program's impact on various educational variables, making use of statistical tools and methods to make sure that the observed effects were most likely due to the program, rather than to chance or other factors.

In absolute terms, "the most common reward earned for education was for high attendance" (Miller et al. 2009, p. 6). One could say that was an expected finding in the context of a developed country. Some could even argue that it served as evidence of the need to move beyond attendance-based conditions toward performance-based ones. However, the same report reveals that only 58% of high-school students, 74% of middle-school students, and 72% of elementary school students earned at least one attendance reward throughout the program's first year. Considering that attendance data was automatically provided by the DoE, the percentage of students that reached the 95% attendance mark at least once was not that impressive.

In comparison to the control group, the report found that the program had no significant impact on either attendance or the academic performance of elementary and middle-school students. The effects were only significant at the high-school level, as a greater percentage of Family Rewards' beneficiaries reached the 95% attendance mark and attempted the minimum of 11 credits compared with their control group counterparts[5] (Miller et al. 2009).

Miller et al. (2009) also report on various implementation challenges during the program's first year. Some were quite similar to those faced by CCTs in the developing world, such as payment problems. Early in the program, it was apparent that even in one of the world's largest financial centers, there were families that did not have access to the banking system. Partnerships were then established with commercial banks, so that beneficiaries could open their bank accounts and incur no additional charge. Even so, during the first year various difficulties were faced due to problems with participants' bank accounts. As a result, 6.5% of

Table 4.3   Third year's set of education-related conditions per school level[a]

School level	Incentivized activities	Rewards
Elementary school	Child scores a level 3 or 4 or improves an ELA or Math test score by one level over the previous year	Grades 3–5: families earn $300 per ELA and Math test
	Parent attends a parent–teacher meeting	$25
Middle school	Child scores a level 3 or 4 or improves an ELA or Math test score by one level over the previous year	Grades 6–8: families earn $350 per ELA and Math test
	Parent attends a parent–teacher meeting	$25
High school	Minimum attendance of 95% of school days during a two-month period	$100
	Student passes a Regents exam, scoring 65 or above	$600 for each of five Regents exams
	Parent attends a parent–teacher meeting	$25
	Student takes the PSAT (Preliminary Scholastic Assessment Test)	$50
	Student accumulates 11 credits in the year	$600
	Student graduates and accumulates 44 credits	$400

[a]Opportunity NYC Family Rewards (2010)

beneficiary families did not receive any payments although they had complied with some activities and earned rewards (Miller et al. 2009).

On the other hand, Opportunity NYC faced some singular difficulties that are worth mentioning. First, since the program went after families rather than the other way around, there were problems finding people. Due to the high mobility of the targeted population, the contact information provided by the DoE was outdated for some families and they could never be reached (Miller et al. 2009).

In addition, Family Rewards' higher complexity in terms of its set of conditionalities and means of verification required the adoption of two peculiar strategies. First, a marketing campaign was developed by a marketing firm with the aim of bringing to participants "catchy" information on how families were expected to participate. Second, individualized bimonthly statements were mailed to families after each payment cycle, highlighting the rewards that a certain family could have earned.

In 2010, MDRC released Opportunity NYC's comprehensive impact evaluation, which covers the first two years of implementation and includes all areas in which the program was expected to have an impact, such as income, education, health, and work.

In education, the report confirmed findings obtained by Miller et al. (2009) for the program's first year of implementation. No impact was found on elementary and middle-school students' attendance or achievement records. Noteworthy impacts were only found among high-school students. Particularly, it was confirmed that Opportunity NYC increased the percentage of students that attempted 11 credits and that took at least one Regents exam. However, this effect of increased student effort was not found to have translated into higher achievement, as the program did not lead to more students *earning* 11 credits or *passing* the Regents (Riccio et al. 2010).

The only educational impacts of Opportunity NYC that were statistically significant and of a considerable magnitude were those found among ninth graders who had scored at or above proficiency level on standardized tests in the eighth grade. Among these, the report highlights the following:

> These include a 6 percentage point reduction in the proportion of students who repeated the ninth grade, a 15 percentage point increase in the likelihood of having a 95 percent or better attendance rate (in Year 2), an 8 percentage point increase in the likelihood of earning at least 22 credits (11 credits per year are needed to remain on track for on-time graduation), and an increase of 6 percentage points in the likelihood of passing at least two Regents exams. (Riccio et al. 2010, p. ES. 14)

The report explains that proficient ninth graders might have been in a better position to take advantage of program incentives and make some educational improvements. However, it should be noted that even among proficient students, these small positive effects were not observed for Math or English language test scores, which was the initial hope of program designers.

In 2013, MDRC released a new follow-up report, this time including findings from the program's third year of operation. The findings were summarized as follows:

1. Reduced current poverty and material hardship, including hunger and some housing-related hardships, although these effects weakened after the cash transfers ended.
2. Helped parents increase savings and reduce reliance on families and friends for cash loans.
3. Did not improve school outcomes overall for elementary or middle-school students, perhaps in part because, for these children, the program rewarded attendance (which was already high) and standardized test scores (rather than more immediate performance such as good report card grades).
4. Had few effects on school outcomes for high-school students overall, but substantially increased graduation rates and other outcomes for students who entered high school as proficient readers.
5. Did not increase families' use of preventive medical care, which was already high, and had few effects on health outcomes.
6. Substantially increased families' receipt of preventive dental care.
7. Increased the likelihood of self-reported full-time employment but did not increase employment in or earnings from jobs covered by the unemployment insurance system (Riccio et al. 2013, p. iii).

At least in education, Opportunity NYC fell short of expectations in its ability of improving educational outcomes by means of the provision of cash rewards. Results were mostly limited to school attendance, just like in most other CCT programs. The following findings on the limited role played by the DoE on the program's design and implementation may be part of the story behind the disappointing results.

4.4   OPPORTUNITY NYC AND EDUCATION POLICIES

As part of their human capital orientation and as illustrated in Chap. 2, conditional cash transfers are expected to include an educational component, even if only at the school attendance level. For a program to be a CCT, it is assumed that it will have education-related conditions, so as to contribute to building human capital and breaking the intergenerational cycle of poverty. Despite their educational "soul," data collected

for Opportunity NYC indicate that the involvement of education authorities, professionals, and scholars in the policymaking and implementation
of CCTs cannot be taken for granted.

In the case of Family Rewards, its design process involved various
meetings with staff members of CEO, MDRC, Seedco, city agencies,
the World Bank, and scholars like Prof. Roland Fryer. The DoE was particularly invited to help determine which education activities should be
incentivized. However, the idea of including performance-based conditionalities actually came from Prof. Roland Fryer, who at the time had
already proposed an incentives-based program for NYC public schools.
The contribution of DoE representatives on that matter was simply the
identification of cutoff points that would be used as thresholds for test
performance.

In those first program design meetings, DoE representatives also
insisted that the program should only reward activities that the department had data for. Kids should not have to do much to demonstrate
compliance and the payment of rewards should be based on objective
information. Consequently, they were against proposals of having students submit "report cards" based on their schools' own grading system.

DoE representatives also advocated for elements that ended up making Family Rewards operate in a significantly different way compared to
Spark: they argued that schools should not be involved, so that students
who were program beneficiaries would not be pointed out and teachers
would not have to carry the burden of making sure that students would
be able to get rewards.

However, after being considerably engaged in defining some "nuts and
bolts" of Family Rewards, DoE participation receded. The department's
engagement in Family Rewards was a lot more significant in the design
stage of the program. After that, the DoE's role was limited to data
reporting for the automatic verification of education-related conditions.

As for Spark, it was never truly owned by the DoE. The lack of integration between Spark and the DoE's policies seems to have been justified on the basis that the program was just an experiment. It was worth
trying, but it was not considered necessary to coordinate it with other
policies because it was still to be seen whether the program would work
or not. In the beginning, at least some Spark staff members were housed
at the DoE. However, with the creation of Opportunity NYC and the
transformation of Spark into one of its subprograms, even that link
ceased to exist.

When one looks deeper into Opportunity NYC, it turns out that part of it, Family Rewards, received initial inputs from the DoE, but the department later came to play a very secondary role in the program's operation and evaluation. As for the other part, Spark, the DoE was not only absent from the program's life, but it actually did not consider Spark to be one of its own initiatives.

The DoE's removed position in relation to Opportunity NYC is most likely the result of a combination of factors. First, the idea of introducing a CCT program did not come from inside the Department, which may have decreased the motivation for involvement. Second, Spark was designed and implemented in such a centralized manner that there was not much demand for participation by DoE's staff. Third, although the department was quite engaged in helping design Family Rewards, it indirectly chose to have a limited participation during the implementation of the program. The DoE's determination that schools should not be involved in Family Rewards ended up removing the program's daily operation from the environment where education policies play out. And fourth, Opportunity NYC's experimental nature to some extent put the department's involvement on stand-by, that is, the DoE was not willing to make much effort until it was clear whether the program worked or not.

Additionally, an interesting observation that arose out of the various interviews was the fact that those involved in Opportunity NYC do not have an educational background, while those who do work with education declared not to know much about the program. Media coverage was an example of such a disconnect between the program and education. Of the 209 newspaper articles that were published on Opportunity NYC from 2007 to 2009, only 19 (9.09%) were indexed as belonging to an education subject.

Added to the above, it seems that education scholars have been particularly disengaged from debating on the program. Among all scholarly journals with editions available through Jstor, only Science and the Harvard Education Letter published articles involving it in the period between 2007 and 2010. The Science article notes that "the program has drawn plenty of flak. The notion of paying for better test scores has raised concerns about the kind of rote learning that it may encourage" (Kaiser 2008). Despite that observation, Kaiser provides a generally positive picture of conditional cash transfers, of which Opportunity NYC is an example. In the Harvard Education Letter, Wilson (2009) attempts to present a balanced perspective of what Spark can do for student motivation. It presents criticisms raised by scholars from the social sciences and from psychology, but none from education scholars.

4.4.1   Advocacy Coalitions

In order to identify whether CCTs may have induced change in education policies by inducing the replacement of the dominating advocacy coalition, this research first tried to identify what competing coalitions existed around education policies in NYC at the time when Opportunity NYC was implemented. Again, according to True et al. (2007), advocacy coalitions are "composed of people from various governmental and private organizations that both (1) share a set of normative and causal beliefs and (2) engage in a nontrivial degree of coordinated activity over time" (p. 120). The present research did not have the ambition of identifying each and every existing advocacy coalition that played a role in education policymaking in the city at the time. However, it was able to identify that the dominating coalition, as represented by the Bloomberg administration, did face competition from at least two other coalitions.

The above finding was based on the idea that the bonding element of a coalition is its "belief system," which is comprised by "value priorities, perceptions about causal relationships, perceptions of world states (including the magnitude of the problem), and perceptions of the efficacy of policy instruments" (pp. 119–120). In order to get to the "deep core," "policy core beliefs," and "secondary aspects" of each coalition's belief system (Sabatier and Jenkins-Smith 1999), interviewees were asked about the main value of education, the city's core educational problems, and its education policy priorities. After contrasting various answers, one can observe a striking but expected difference between the points of view espoused by the DoE, the United Federation of Teachers (UFT), and the "conservatives",[6] respectively:

> [The main value of education] is to prepare students to be successful once they graduate from high school, whether that means moving on to college of if that means to be able to successfully compete in the workforce. (interviewee A12)

> Education enables people to improve the quality of their lives, both intellectually and financially to problem solve, to address issues in their communities, in their nation, around the world, to be productive citizens in a global economy. (interviewee A1)

[The main value of education] is not just financial or economic. It enriches your life to have a good well-grounded education in history, in literature, to know how to do some basic mathematical calculations so that you can understand when the newspaper is misrepresenting statistics. I think it is a good idea to have a good grounding so that you can be a productive member of society in general, in all areas. I mean, everyone should know something about science, evolution, math, those basic foundations of literature. (...) And then, of course, it's beneficial for society. (interviewee A5)

Their views were also distinct in regard to the city's major educational problems. For the DoE these problems mostly comprise low graduation rates in high school, issues of school safety, and being able to deliver quality education in an equitable way. The UFT rather emphasizes the lack of adequate resources, especially the kind of intensive support services that most disadvantaged children need. Contrary to this view, the conservatives argue that NYC's main educational problem is definitely not lack of money. The blame is actually directed to unions, which have been resistant to kids going to school all day and during the summer, and parents, who do not provide the necessary support to their kids' school life.

Hence, there is on the DoE's side a pragmatic and almost functionalist belief system, whose policy priorities are "accountability, empowerment and leadership" (interviewee A12). Commenting on the administration's position, the UFT staff member said "the vision today is more results-oriented, more corporate-minded. (...) The administration believes that they don't care about how you produce the results, they want to see the text scores" (interviewee A1). On the other hand, the UFT itself presents a belief system that is concerned about the multiple facets of education, that sees lack of resources as the seed of all problems, and that is against the culture of testing. "The art of testing is not well-developed enough yet to capture any of the things that teachers teach aside from the subjects. (...) Scholars pretty much agree that tests are simply not developed, not reliable enough to base high stakes decisions" (interviewee A1). Finally, conservative voices put the blame on "dysfunctional" families and on strong unions, arguing that the government is already doing more than it should.

As a policy solution, Opportunity NYC—with its straightforward logic of paying for better test results—fits well into the belief system that was advocated and practiced by the DoE since the time when school chancellor Joel Klein took office. Thus, the interplay between different advocacy coalitions concerned about education in New York City does not seem to have been altered by the introduction of Opportunity NYC. If anything, the program reinforced the status quo. As a consequence, one can say that the program was not in a position to induce policy change in education, since in order to accomplish that it would be necessary to "affect the constraints and opportunities of subsystem actors" (Sabatier and Jenkins-Smith 1999, p. 120) and allow for the replacement of the coalition that dominated education policies.

4.5 POLITICAL SUSTAINABILITY: IT IS AN EXPERIMENT

Opportunity NYC initially appeared to differ from other CCTs because it suffered from some harsh criticisms that had been published by the press. Below are some examples:

> The political spectrum united to oppose the whole idea. The Manhattan Institute's Sol Stern said paying for test performance undermined learning for its own sake. New York University historian Diane Ravitch called it "anti-democratic, anti-civic, anti-intellectual, and anti-social". Leo Casey of the United Federation of Teachers objected that "money can't buy you learning." On his show, Stephen Colbert teased city schools Chancellor Joel I. Klein, "As long as you're going to be paying kids and making it seem like a job, why not just bring back child labor? (Kahlenberg 2007)

> While Opportunity NYC has its fans, some observers regard it as abhorrent. Heather Mac Donald wrote that cash for behavior "will further shorten the poor's time horizon, rather than lengthen it." She regards the rewarded activities as things that parents and students should do on their own because they understand the value of behaving properly—not as a response to government intervention. Furthermore, she envisions that low-income families not enrolled in the program will resent that they are not being paid and will be less motivated to do the right things. (Liebling 2007)

These initial manifestations of opinion, as soon as Opportunity NYC started operating, created doubts of whether it would survive so much opposition. Even the administration acknowledged that the program was "too innovative almost" by funding it exclusively with private resources. The Mayor's bet was that if the program was able to demonstrate positive results, they would speak for themselves and would silence opposing voices.

With that in mind, this research attempted to analyze Opportunity NYC's political sustainability through the lenses of the punctuated-equilibrium theory (PET) and the civic capacity theoretical framework. PET argues that the policy process is comprised by long periods of policy continuity that are followed by bursts of policy change. It explains continuity (or lack of change) as the result of a policy monopoly, which is "a monopoly on political understandings concerning the policy of interest and an institutional arrangement that reinforces that understanding" (Baumgartner and Jones 1993, p. 6). Policy monopolies are controlled by government institutions that constitute "policy venues," but are maintained thanks to a positive and well-accepted policy image. The policy image is the "prevalent understanding of the policy" (Baumgartner and Jones 1993, p. 7).

Baumgartner and Jones (1993) identified policy monopolies over long periods of time. It is thus unlikely that Opportunity NYC might have consolidated its own policy monopoly during its three years of experimental existence. Furthermore, education policies have not been dominated by an incentive-for-effort rationale (at least as far as students are concerned), nor have welfare policies abandoned their traditional practices of case management and unconditional assistance. Therefore, analyzing Opportunity NYC's political sustainability meant analyzing its potential of forming a new policy monopoly, especially in the field of social welfare.

This research was able to find that some of the main necessary variables for policy change and the consolidation of a new policy monopoly by Opportunity NYC—according to PET—were in place. Attention and a positive policy image were some of those elements. According to the Dow Jones Factiva database, from 01 January 2007 to 31 December 2009, Opportunity NYC was featured in 208 newspaper articles around the world, 168 of them having been published in the US and 97 in NYC papers. Besides, 65 included the word successful within their text. Heightened public attention and media attention have been identified by True, et al. (2007) as part of the process by which an issue moves higher in the political agenda, eventually leading to policy change.

At least until the release of its evaluation report, Opportunity NYC's policy image had been strong and positive. Beyond any questions of agreement or disagreement with the program's fundamentals, its policy image was related to the idea of an experiment and of evidence-based policymaking. Its experimental image was strategically cultivated by the institutions that were responsible for the program. In every interview, their representatives emphasized that Opportunity NYC was an experiment and that in the worst scenario it would "add to our base knowledge" (interviewee A7). Interviewee A11 specifically argued that they had been able to diffuse critics because the program did not involve public dollars and because it was a full-scale research project. As there is a dominating belief that experimenting is always desirable and that evidence-based policymaking is the gold standard, Opportunity NYC counted on the credential of being a legitimate policy attempt to reach results through the test of an innovative solution. The following excerpts are examples of that:

> I think that it is an intriguing enough and sexy enough program that if it is promising it will continue, especially if Bloomberg continues as Mayor. (…) I think it will keep going if it can show that the pilot, the evaluation is positive. (…) It really depends on the evaluation. (interviewee A2)

> These findings suggest that policy experimentation and innovation is important to increase the impact of CCTs on learning outcomes. Experimentation would be valuable on a number of fronts, such as different bundles of intervention. (Fiszbein and Schady 2009, p. 143).

In terms of civic capacity,[7] this research was not able to conclude whether the school community, parents, and local leaders had actively supported Opportunity NYC. However, it was able to determine that potential opponents had not mobilized resources to impede the continuation of the program.

Despite what seemed to be a polarization of opinions around Opportunity NYC—as portrayed by the media in the beginning—those who could oppose it did not get organized. The members of conservative think tanks who believe that "the City of New York should not compare its conditions to CCTs in Latin America" (interviewee A5) did not go beyond publishing opinion editorials against the program.

As for the United Federation of Teachers, which would be expected to mount some opposition to the idea of cash-for-performance, it did not take an official position on cash rewards. In fact, the UFT interviewee argued that teachers use rewards all the time: class parties, candies, points, stars, and class trips. For her the whole idea of rewards is not new and she personally does not have anything against using cash. What she is critical of is the use of tests as the means to assess progress and define who merits to be rewarded. That is consistent with the over-all belief system she subscribes to, which does not seem to be contrary to incentivizing learning. For her, the administration may have a hard time justifying the program. The reasons, however, are not to be found in political or ideological differences, but rather in the difficult budget climate of the moment (interviewee A1).

Added to the lack of mobilization by potential opponents, data analysis conducted on newspapers published between early 2007 and late 2009 identified that, despite the initially heated debate, of 168[8] articles published in the US only 17 (10.11%) included the word "controversial" and 18 (10.71%) the word "critics." That is another sign that the program was not as disputed as first expected by this study and by City Hall.

Therefore, with its policy image closely linked to the idea of evidence-based policymaking and no organized opposition to it, Opportunity NYC should have been able to survive. Why did it not? Why was it ended in 2010? The answer goes back exactly to the program's policy image. Opportunity NYC was directly connected with the idea of experimentation. As such, there was an underlying promise that it would not be scaledup or continued if the relevant results were not reached. And as discussed earlier in this chapter, the evaluation results were far from glooming. Significant impacts were minimal and did not signal that it would be worth it investing public resources in the Opportunity NYC model, at least as it had been tried out.

As published by the New York Times right after the evaluation report was released in 2010:

> When the mayor announced the program, he said it would begin with private money and, if it worked, could be transformed into an ambitious permanent government program. But city officials said Tuesday that there were no specific plans at this time to go forward with a publicly financed version of the program. (Bosman 2010)

Interestingly, the program reached a positive and strong policy image due to its experimental nature and the dominating discourse around evidence-based policymaking. Curiously, it was that policy image that made it doomed for termination, only three years after much visibility and glamor.

It should be pointed out, however, that a "derivation" of Opportunity NYC—Family Rewards has survived in what MDRC has called demonstration projects or Family Rewards 2.0 (Riccio et al. 2013). According to the 2013 evaluation report, a modified version of Family Rewards was being tried at a smaller scale in Memphis, Tennessee, and the Bronx, New York. This time, however, it has counted on federal funding from the Social Innovation Fund:

> The new model targets low-income families with children in grades 9 and 10 only, rather than including children in elementary and middle school, as in the original program. It offers fewer rewards, disburses payments more frequently, and rewards report card grades in addition to attendance and test scores to provide a more immediate incentive for better school performance. It also adds a family guidance component. It is hoped that this refined version of Family Rewards will be more effective than the original program. (Riccio et al. 2013, pp. xiii–xiv)

Hence, the program did not survive long enough to be turned into a public policy and consequently make its own policy monopoly in New York City. However, it did survive as a policy option, one that has caught the attention of researchers and federal authorities, at least to the point of motivating new experimentations.

4.6 POLICY DIFFUSION: REALLY BORROWED FROM MEXICO?

Opportunity NYC has been announced and advertised as an import from Mexico. CEO's 2009 annual report brings a section titled "From Oportunidades to Opportunity NYC," suggesting that the New York program was named after its Mexican inspiration. According to the World Bank's latest book on CCTs, "Opportunity NYC was modeled explicitly on Mexico's Oportunidades" (Fiszbein and Schady 2009, p. 144). Additionally, among the 209 newspaper articles found on Opportunity NYC, 109 (52.15%) make reference to Mexico and 76 (36.36%) to *Oportunidades*.

In the early stages of the New York program, there were indeed numerous exchanges between Opportunity NYC's designers and *Oportunidades'* officials. Joint workshops and study tours were organized. However, if one looks at how the two programs operate, it becomes apparent that Opportunity NYC has preserved only a few characteristics of its Mexican counterpart. It also diverges from the Brazilian and the Bogota experiences in many respects, as shown in the following chapters.

At the discourse level, Opportunity NYC kept the ideas of breaking the intergenerational cycle of poverty and of investing in human capital. Nonetheless, if one compares its documents with international papers and reports on CCTs, it is interesting to notice how different the language used is. Whereas CCT experts in Mexico, Brazil, Colombia, and other countries talk about "conditionalities" and "stipends" (*bolsa* in Portuguese, *bono* or *subsidio* in Spanish), Opportunity NYC has "activities" and "rewards" or "incentives." Opportunity NYC interviewees used expressions such as "customer service," "reward menu," and "claims processing," which were not part of the language used by *Bolsa Familia's* and *Subsidios'* interviewees. The open and direct reference to reducing poverty and inequality is also subtle in Opportunity NYC, which rather insists on "behavior change" and "creating opportunities." Hence, if one considers the distinction between "policy talk," "policy action," and "policy implementation" (Tyack and Cuban 1995), the kind of policy borrowing that took place in Opportunity NYC has not been complete even at the minimum level of policy talk, being closer to what the literature calls "brand-name piracy" (Steiner-Khamsi 2004).

When it comes to program operations, Opportunity NYC has preserved two features of CCTs: they are targeted rather than universal programs, and use cash. Targeting in New York involved three phases: geographic targeting, income-based targeting,[9] and then a lottery system. The program delivered payments directly to bank accounts, making it possible for beneficiaries to withdraw them with an ATM card. That feature is also becoming increasingly common among other CCTs.

However, differences in terms of program operations abound. First, there was a deliberate process of searching for eligible families and having them apply to the lottery. In most CCTs, there are only public information campaigns to let eligible families know that they should apply. Program managers do not go after families to convince them to participate. Second, the hiring of NPOs to do the recruitment work and support families throughout the program was also a different feature. In only a few CCTs, local women are hired or volunteer to support beneficiaries, but they obviously count on more limited resources.

Additionally, as mentioned above, Opportunity NYC had a long list of conditionalities and families only received payments if they were able to properly hand in coupons to prove compliance. Again, these aspects added complexity to the program and made it more time-consuming for participating families.

The above comparison makes it clear that although there has been great emphasis on following the Mexican experience and on South–North learning, Opportunity NYC was a singular experiment compared with most existing CCTs. The reasons behind that deviation from the standard CCT *modus operandi* may have to do with the fact that the program was not dependent upon international funding. Therefore, it did not need to strictly follow the "global CCT model."

Also, it looks like there is in the US a different understanding about the causes of poverty and how it should be tackled. Whereas internationally these reasons are seen as structural, related to the history and development of each country, in the US they are approached as a consequence of individual effort and behavior. That may be why Opportunity NYC was less about providing additional income to poor families—as in the case of *Oportunidades, Bolsa Familia,* and others—and more about incentivizing behavior.

The emphasis that was given to the idea that Opportunity NYC borrowed its policy model from Mexico can be explained by the borrowing and lending literature through the concepts of "externalization" and "certification strategy" (Steiner-Khamsi 2004). According to that literature, governments declare to borrow policy models from other countries in order to legitimize policy ideas that have been domestically grown. As previously reported, the proposal of an incentives program to induce behavior, such as improved academic performance, had already been introduced in the US by Prof. Roland Fryer. But as Spark was included under the umbrella of Opportunity NYC, it became part of the "borrowing from Mexico" package and consequently received the certification and legitimization that comes with policy borrowing from elsewhere.

Also, as City Hall expected to face opposition to its incentive program, it used the reference to *Oportunidades* as a shield. Interestingly, the "borrowing from Mexico" idea backfired and ended up being also criticized, with many pointing the finger at how poverty conditions were different in New York City compared to rural Mexico (Gelinas 2006). Consequently, program managers had to eventually emphasize that they were aware of the contextual differences and that adaptations had been duly carried out. The following paragraph from Opportunity NYC's evaluation report exemplifies this process:

In 2006, mindful of the differences between Mexico's rural poor (where the most evidence had been amassed) and the urban poor in this country, but impressed by the success of Oportunidades and other countries' CCT programs, Mayor Michael Bloomberg's Center for Economic Opportunity (CEO) began to explore whether a CCT program could be adapted for use in New York City's poorest neighborhoods. (Riccio et al. 2010)

4.7   NEVER TOO EARLY FOR POLICY DIFFUSION?

Interestingly, there were efforts to disseminate the Opportunity NYC experience since the early stages of the program's pilot, even in the absence of evidence of its impact. According to the borrowing and lending literature, this suggests an attempt to obtain legitimacy for the program through policy lending (Steiner-Khamsi 2004). As other countries import its model, it is used as proof of the program's value.

Why would Opportunity NYC need to be legitimized? First, because the media initially created the impression that the program was too controversial. Second, because the continuation or replication of Opportunity NYC after the three-year pilot would depend on public funding.

In December 2007, only three months after Opportunity NYC started operating, the city government participated in a UN Conference on South–South learning. A few months later, the Rockefeller Foundation gave a grant to MDRC in order to establish the Conditional Cash Transfer Learning Network, whose purpose was to allow other cities and countries to learn from the Opportunity NYC experience (interviewee A9). During the launch of the network, Mayor Bloomberg said:

> We are encouraged by the interest generated in Opportunity NYC, and look forward to sharing our expertise with others as they seek to tackle the issue of poverty in their respective countries and cities. (Rockefeller Foundation 2008)

In the framework of the CCT learning network, the Rockefeller Foundation funded a seminar on CCT experiences in July 2008. The seminar brought to Rockefeller's Bellagio Center in Italy CCT experts from several countries, including Colombia, Brazil, Indonesia, Turkey, and South Africa. Representatives of the World Bank, Seedco, CEO, MDRC, and EdLabs were also present.

Later in 2009, another initiative that would work as a platform to help disseminate New York City's experience was created: the Inter-American Social Protection Network (IASPN). "The objective of the IASPN is to promote cooperation and information-sharing among countries and institutions on social protection practices that provide real solutions to help reduce social inequality and poverty" (Organization of American States 2009). During the launch of the IASPN, Secretary of State Hillary Clinton praised CCTs for their impact on reducing poverty and inequality (Organization of American States 2009).

Interestingly, Opportunity NYC's managers and funders readily listed the program's "best practice" elements, although evaluation results had been made available only recently. Interviewees from CEO, MDRC, the Rockefeller Foundation, and the World Bank were unanimous about the set of program aspects that they considered innovative and that could inform policies in other cities and countries: the work component; incentives for academic performance; established alliances with local organizations for family guidance; and the operation in a large urban setting (interviewees A7, A8, A9, and A10).

Mayor Bloomberg, in his words of endorsement to the World Bank's most recent book on CCTs, said: "We look forward to adding our evaluation results to an important body of research and continuing our work with partners worldwide to reach our shared goal of breaking the cycles of intergenerational poverty" (Bloomberg, quoted in Fiszbein and Schady 2009, back cover).

Opportunity NYC's lending drive was met with much enthusiasm by the international community. Program managers were invited to present the New York experience at international meetings, such as the one organized in Cartagena, Colombia, in September 2008. The meeting, called International Seminar on CCTs in Urban Areas, counted on the participation of Deputy Mayor Linda Gibbs and Seedco's Executive Vice-President Andrea Phillips.

Additionally, the World Bank, which was initially an important source of CCT expertise during the design of Opportunity NYC, turned into a main bridge for its lending to other countries. For instance, the bank organized study tours for foreign delegations to get to learn from the New York experience. That was the case of a visit by a Nigerian delegation and of a workshop with representatives of Latin American countries (Chile, Colombia, Mexico, and Brazil) in June 2009. According to the bank's main book on CCTs:

In the United States there is some experience with programs that pay for final outcomes rather than for service use. Given the concerns about whether CCT programs in developing countries are succeeding in improving final outcomes (for example, learning outcomes), experimentation with alternative incentive schemes (perhaps through small-scale pilot programs) is justified. (Fiszbein and Schady 2009, p. 179)

Interestingly, the New York CCT experience left some interesting lessons in terms of policy diffusion. First, a program can be called a "best practice" before anyone knows for sure that it is really the best. Second, international actors can play an important role in policy diffusion and "best practice" promotion even—or should one say especially—when the model comes from the North. Finally, there is always much talk about a policy innovation, but not so much dissemination of information about a program's misdeeds, so much so that little has been said about Opportunity NYC since 2010.

The following chapter will be dedicated to another city-based CCT program, however, one that has reached interesting connections with the educational sector. It brings a completely new policy story, one about which little has been known in the CCT world.

NOTES

1. Currently, MDRC is no longer an acronym. It used to stand for Manpower Demonstration Research Corporation.
2. Seedco is no longer an acronym. It used to stand for Structured Employment Economic Development Corporation.
3. "Central and East Harlem in Manhattan; Brownsville and East New York in Brooklyn; and Morris Heights/Mount Hope and East Tremont/Belmont in the Bronx" (MDRC 2008, p. 3).
4. Being eligible for free lunch or reduced-price lunch was used as evidence of low-income status.
5. Although not all of those beneficiary students successfully completed attempted credits.
6. As represented by the interviews with members of a conservative think tank in the City.
7. According to Stone et al. (2001) civic capacity can be defined as "the involvement of various sectors of the community in a problem-solving effort" (p. 20).

8. This number does not include media coverage of the program's impact evaluation.
9. Although this was done through education data (children eligible for reduced-price lunch) rather than through a means test.

REFERENCES

Baumgartner, F., & Jones, B. (1993). *Agendas and instability in American politics.* Chicago: University of Chicago Press.

Bosman, J. (2009, September 20). Cash incentive program for poor families is renewed. *The New York Times.* Retrieved December 19, 2009, from http://www.nytimes.com/2009/09/21/nyregion/21opportunity.html?scp=1&sq=Cash%20incentives%20program%20for%20poor%20families%20is%20renewed&st=cse.

Bosman, J. (2010, March 30). City will stop paying the poor for good behavior. *The New York Times.* Retrieved March 31, 2010, from http://www.nytimes.com/2010/03/31/nyregion/31cash.html?hp.

Center for Economic Opportunity. (2009). *Early achievements and lessons learned.* New York: Center for Economic Opportunity.

Center for Economic Opportunity, MDRC , Seedco. (2008, November 6). *Testing Conditional Cash Transfer (CCT) Programs in New York City. Family rewards demonstration.* Presentation at the Association for Public Policy Analysis and Management Annual Meetings, Los Angeles.

Dubner, S. (2005, March 20). Toward a unified theory of black America. *New York Times Magazine.* Retrieved July 15, 2008, from http://www.nytimes.com/2005/03/20/magazine/20HARVARD.html?pagewanted=all.

Education Innovation Laboratory. (2010). *About us.* Retrieved January 12, 2010, from http://www.edlabs.harvard.edu/.

Fiszbein, A., & Schady, N. (2009). *Conditional cash transfers: Reducing present and future poverty.* Washington, DC: The World Bank Group.

Gelinas, N. (2006). New York isn't Mexico. *City Journal, 17*(4). Retrieved October 25, 2007, from http://www.city-journal.org/html/eon2006-10-20ng.html.

Kaiser, J. (2008). Money—with strings—to fight poverty. *Science, 319*(5864), 754–755.

Kahlenberg, R. (2007). In defense of Bloomberg's bribe. *Slate Magazine.* Retrieved January 4, 2008, from http://www.slate.com/id/2177554/.

Liebling, B. (2007). *Sometimes, cash incentives can hurt.* Retrieved November 28, 2007, from http://www.american.com/archive/2007/july-0707/sometimes-cash-incentives-can-hurt/.

MDRC. (2008). *Program design and evaluation strategy for opportunity NYC – Family Rewards. A comprehensive conditional cash transfer (CCT) pilot program for New York City.* Unpublished manuscript.

Miller, C., Riccio, J., & Smith, J. (2009). *A preliminary look at early educational results of the Opportunity NYC – Family Rewards program. A research note for funders.* Unpublished manuscript.

Office of the Mayor. (2007). *Mayor Bloomberg Welcomes First Opportunity NYC Programm Participants and Announces Partnerships with Eight Local Banks and Credit Unions to Offer Them "No Fee" Accounts.* Retrieved October 20, 2007, from http://www.nyc.gov/portal/site/nycgov/menuitem.c0935b9a5 7bb4ef3daf2f1c701c789a0/index.jsp?pageID=mayor_press_ release&catID=1194&doc_name=http%3A%2F%2Fwww.nyc.gov%2Fhtml% 2Fom%2Fhtml%2F2007b%2Fpr33007.html&cc=unused1978&rc=1194& ndi=1.

Opportunity NYC Family Rewards. (2010). *Education rewards.* Retrieved January 15, 2010, from http://www.opportunitynyc.org/?q=education.

Organization of American States. (2009, October). Inter-American Social Protection Network launched. *Summit of the Americas Newsletter.* Retrieved January 6, 2010, from http://www.summit-americas.org/Newsletter/2009/ nl_en_1009_iaspn.htm.

Riccio, J., Dechausay, N., Greenberg, D., Miller, C., Rucks, Z., & Verma, N. (2010). *Toward reduced poverty across generations: Early findings from New York City's Conditional Cash Transfer program.* Retrieved March 30, 2010, from http://www.mdrc.org/publications/549/full.pdf.

Riccio, J., Dechausay, N., Miller, C., Nuñez, S., Verma, N., & Yang, E. (2013). *Conditional Cash Transfers in New York City: The continuing story of the Opportunity NYC – Family Rewards demonstration.* New York: MDRC.

Rockefeller Foundation. (2008). *Mayor Bloomberg and the Rockefeller Foundation announce the launch of a learning network to share design and implementation of a conditional cash transfer program.* Retrieved January 24, 2010, from http://www.rockefellerfoundation.org/news/press-releases/mayor-bloomb-erg-rockefeller-foundation.

Sabatier, P., & Jenkins-Smith, P. (1999). The advocacy coalition framework: An assessment. In P. Sabatier (Ed.), *Theories of the policy process.* Boulder: Westview Press.

Steiner-Khamsi, G. (2004). *The politics of educational borrowing and lending.* New York: Teachers College Press.

Stone, C., Henig, J., Jones, B., & Pierannunzi, C. (2001). *Building civic capacity: The politics of reforming urban schools.* Lawrence: University Press of Kansas.

True, J., Jones, B., & Baumgartner, F. (2007). Punctuated-equilibrium theory: Explaining stability and change in American policymaking. In P. Sabatier (Ed.), *Theories of the policy process.* Boulder: Westview Press.

Tyack, D., & Cuban, L. (1995). *Tinkering toward utopia: A century of public school reform.* Cambridge, MA: Harvard University Press.

UN Webcast Archives (2007). *Eyes on the South as a Knowledge Hub.* Retrieved November 25, 2007, from http://www.un.org/webcast/SE2007.html.

Wilson, D. M. (2009). Money and motivation. *Harvard Education Newsletter, 35*(2). Retrieved January 23, 2010, from http://www.hepg.org/hel/article/162.

CHAPTER 5

Money to Bear the Indirect Costs of Schooling

In 2004, Bogota's Secretary of Education, Abel Rodriguez, got acquainted with a study of the city's main educational problems and needs. The assessment had been prepared by an independent consultant, who identified that Bogota's core educational bottleneck was the high dropout rate in lower and upper secondary school. Despite superior net enrollment in basic education (85% in primary education and 80% in secondary), Bogota faces severe dropout problems. In 2003, it was estimated that there were 89,000 dropouts among children and adolescents, 98% of them being from SISBEN[1] 1 and 2, or the poorest social strata (IDB 2005). According to the World Bank (2006), low completion of secondary school is actually a national problem:

> The country [Colombia] has increased net primary enrollment to roughly 90 percent, approaching the regional average, and has both reduced primary repetition and increased primary completion. Colombia has also increased net secondary enrollment to 65 percent, which, though considerably below primary enrollment, also approaches the regional average. Colombia is now tasked with improving education quality and equity and increasing secondary completion rates. (p. vii)

With that assessment in mind, the Education Secretary decided to hire the consultant to help his team design a pilot program that would tackle the dropout issue. The consultant, who had just returned from doing a Master's program in the US, was highly interested in testing a program

© The Author(s) 2017   103
M. Morais de Sá e Silva, *Poverty Reduction, Education, and the Global Diffusion of Conditional Cash Transfers*, DOI 10.1007/978-3-319-53094-9_5

with the following three characteristics: (1) a pilot that could be implemented as a randomized field trial; (2) a conditional cash transfer with a savings component but without the problems of Mexico's *Jovenes con Oportunidades*[2]; and (3) a program that could be subject to a rigorous impact evaluation. The consultant brought on board experts from the MIT-based Poverty Action Lab, who later put together US-based researchers to work on the program's quantitative evaluation (interviewee A6). Fedesarollo, a local think tank, was also invited to participate in the design of the program.

Coincidentally, the consultant happened to meet on a flight the country director of the Inter-American Development Bank (IDB) in Colombia. He explained to him how the CCT pilot would operate in Bogota. IDB's country director immediately showed an interest in the program and proposed a loan to help fund it. These funds would be included as part of a broader loan that the IDB was about to provide to the city's Department of Education to help build 20 new public schools (interviewee A6).

The pilot program, which was named *Subsidios Condicionados a la Asistencia Escolar*[3] (hereinafter *Subsidios*), started in 2005 and was initially funded by the Department of Education. In December 2006, IDB resources were received: a total of US$ 20.3 million, which lasted until 2009. That budget was part of the overarching "Bogota Equity in Education Program," an IDB loan to the city government of US$ 92.9 million (IDB, 2006).

5.1   SUBSIDIOS' FEATURES

Subsidios was designed to reduce school dropout and increase graduation rates. As indicated above, besides working as a direct intervention, *Subsidios* was initially an experiment, just like Opportunity NYC. It encompassed three payment schemes involving different conditionalities and cash benefits. The idea was to evaluate which scheme would be more effective in keeping beneficiaries in school.

Initially, the program was implemented in only two of the city's 20 districts—Suba and San Cristobal. Interviewee B6 explained the main reason for the choice of geographical targeting: when the program was designed, SISBEN data had been just collected and the results were available only for Suba and San Cristobal; additionally, it was politically desirable to have the program operating in those districts. Although the

IDB loan document tried to justify the choice with poverty indicators, the two districts are not the poorest in Bogota.

As detailed in Mayer and Morais (2008), the different payment schemes were organized into three "modalities":

1. Modality 1: bimonthly transfer of 60,000[4] pesos for up to 2 years for students in the 6th–11th grades in San Cristobal and the 6th–8th grades in Suba.[5]
2. Modality 2: bimonthly transfer of 40,000 pesos plus a yearly saving of 100,000 pesos to be received upon grade completion for up to 2 years. Beneficiary students should be in the 6th – 11th grades and should reside in San Cristobal.
3. Modality 3: bimonthly transfer of 40,000 pesos plus a yearly saving of 100,000 pesos to be received upon grade completion for up to 3 years. Additional 600,000 pesos upon enrollment in postsecondary education. Beneficiary students should be in the 9th – 11th grades and should reside in Suba.

The condition for the transfer of bimonthly payments was class attendance during all schooldays, with the possibility of justified absences due to unforeseen events. Added to that, modalities 2 and 3 had a savings component, where students received a fixed amount of money for grade completion. On top of that, modality 3 had a graduation bonus, which was aimed at encouraging students to graduate from high school, besides giving them the means to start a postsecondary/higher education program.

Initially, the idea was to enroll current students as well as dropouts in the program. A "marketing" campaign was done in the districts through posters, as well as in schools. Despite that, not many out-of-school adolescents presented themselves to register for the program. Since a control group was needed, applications remained open until a sufficient number of candidates—both enrolled and not enrolled in school—were available (interviewee B6). At the end there were 17,818 applications, of which 9749 students were selected through a public lottery event (IDB 2006). The event gathered representatives of the Department of Education, Fedesarollo, parents, school principals, teachers, and other education stakeholders in order to make the selection of participants as transparent as possible.

Different from most Latin American large-scale CCTs (and similar to Spark), the target population of *Subsidios* consisted of students, rather than their families. Consequently, and as the selection of beneficiaries was random, in some cases families with two or more eligible children had just one child benefiting from the program.

Another operational peculiarity of *Subsidios* is that parents had to sign, at the beginning of their child's participation in the program, a document called "terms of commitment," where they declared to be fully aware of the conditionalities to be fulfilled in order to receive cash payments.

By the end of the program's first year of operation, a team of US-based researchers carried out the planned quantitative evaluation. Data were collected in order to compare the control and treatment groups. Among the various findings, the results indicated that modality 3 had the greatest impact. According to Barrera-Osorio et al. (2008), "compared to the basic treatment, the tertiary treatment encourages higher levels of daily attendance (3.5% points more for students least likely to attend) and higher levels of enrollment at the secondary (3.3% points) and tertiary levels (46% points)" (p.6).

Despite these results, in 2006 the Department of Education decided to discontinue modality 3, transferring its beneficiaries to modality 2. According to interviewee B6, the reason was essentially political, since a future bonus payment is not as politically rewarding as bimonthly or end-of-the-year payments. Additionally, the decision was also related to the creation of a new program to support enrollment in postsecondary education, as explained below.

In that same year the DoE also made the decision to expand the *Subsidios* program (modalities 1 and 2) to all districts. However, that scaling-up generated targeting errors (leakage), even though the program's targeting criteria are based on the SISBEN proxy means test. Consequently, it was decided that the next expansion would be carried out only in the poorest *Unidades de Planeamiento Zonal* (Units of Zoning Planning— UPZs). UPZs are territorial portions of the city with certain socioeconomic characteristics. In practice, they are subdivisions of districts, but for planning purposes they have the advantage of being more homogeneous compared with the district as a whole.

In order to better understand the policy context in which the *Subsidios* program operated, it is important to bear in mind the existence of two other programs, which have some characteristics of a CCT and were closely related to *Subsidios*. The first—*Subsidio a la Educación Superior Técnica y Tecnológica* (Subsidy for Technical and Technological Higher Education)—initially benefitted *Subsidios* participants of modality 3. The second—*Subsidio de Transporte* (Transportation Subsidy)—was managed by the same DoE Division as the *Subsidios* program. The existence of the other two programs created some confusion among school principals and coordinators, who had to take stock of the student fulfillment of conditionalities in each program. The implementation of the various "subsidies" was a result of the DoE's policy of tackling school dropouts by financially supporting low-income students.

5.1.1   Subsidy for Technical and Technological Higher Education

A year after the concurrent implementation of the three modalities, a new program was "attached" to the CCT experiment: *Subsidio a la Educación Superior Técnica y Tecnológica* (Subsidy for Technical and Technological Higher Education). In this new program, modality 3 beneficiaries who were in the 11th grade in 2005 and fulfilled the requirement of graduating from high school were offered a full scholarship for postsecondary education starting in 2006. The additional bonus that had been initially promised for enrollment in higher education was replaced by a scholarship covering tuition and stipend for six semesters. Students could choose from a selection of technical and technological careers[6] in a set of private institutions accredited by the city Department of Education (Mayer[7] and Morais 2008).

The first year of the postsecondary scholarship program operated only with modality 3 beneficiaries. Since the program was created during the vacation months and students did not know of its existence, the DoE had to contact each beneficiary by phone and explain that they were being offered a full postsecondary scholarship. Some were not found, whereas others could not accept the offer due to military service, teenage pregnancy, and other personal circumstances (Mayer and Morais 2008).

As a matter of fact, some of the characteristics of the postsecondary scholarship program made it resemble a CCT: payments were conditional upon minimum class attendance and minimum academic performance. Also, the program was an indirect incentive for high-school students to remain in school and graduate. The possibility of having access to a postsecondary scholarship might encourage students who did not have the means to pay for higher education (and therefore could lack in motivation) to graduate from high school.

Different from Opportunity NYC, however, performance was not measured by means of standardized tests, but rather through assessments designed by each professor, in each program, in each postsecondary institution. Naturally, operational difficulties arose, as the participating institutions had different academic calendars and payments were not disbursed until all grades of all beneficiaries had been received. Long payment delays that resulted from these difficulties ended up creating hardships for students, who had to borrow money in order to pay for daily school expenses (Mayer and Morais 2008).

5.1.2   Transportation Subsidy

Besides the *Subsidios Condicionados a la Asistencia Escolar* or *Subsidio Educativo* (Education Subsidy), the Department of Education also ran a program called "*Subsidio de Transporte*" (Transportation Subsidy).

Just like the above scholarship program had some characteristics of a CCT, the transportation subsidy was somewhere in between a CCT and a transportation voucher. Among its CCT features were the conditionalities of not having more than ten class absences throughout the school year and of not having "three reported incidents of misbehavior, indiscipline or aggression in the transportation service" (Secretaria de Educación del Distrito Capital 2010).

The program was targeted at low-income students who lived farther than 2 km from the school where he/she was enrolled. It was a response to the limited capacity of some schools to enroll all students living in their neighborhood. These students ended up needing to be matriculated far from home and to bear with the transportation costs, which for some families was the reason why they would take their children out of school. In 2009 alone, the program benefited 9000 students (interviewee B2).

Table 5.1 was prepared for easier visualization of the CCT-like programs implemented by Bogota's Department of Education.

5.1.3   Program Modifications Along the Way

Since the *Subsidios* program first started operating in 2005, a number of modifications were made to its mode of operation. The first involved

Table 5.1   CCT-like Programs Implemented by Bogota's DoE

	Education subsidy	Postsecondary scholarship program	Transportation subsidy
Target population	SISBEN 2 students enrolled in 6th to 11th grade	SISBEN 1 and 2 graduates from public high schools	Students enrolled in 8th to 11th grade and who live farther than 2 km from school
Conditionalities	No unjustified absences	Minimum class attendance of 80% Minimum score of 3.2 Pass all courses	No more than 10 absences throughout the school year
Maximum duration	2 years	3 years	4 years
Payment amount	70,000 pesos bimonthly or 50,000 bimonthly plus 100,000 by the end of the year	Full tuition and stipend of one minimum salary per month (about US$ 250)	Varies according to price of return bus tickets

the elimination of modality 3 and the scaling-up of modalities 1 and 2, as mentioned above. Additionally, modality 1 became exclusively targeted at grades 9, 10, and 11 whereas modality 2 was directed to students in grades 6, 7, and 8. Payment amounts were also increased, so as to cope with the effects of inflation. Modality 1 payments were turned into 70,000 pesos every two months, whereas modality 2 beneficiaries received 50,000 bimonthly and could save 20,000 for the end of the school year, which would result in a yearly savings of 100,000 pesos[8] (interviewee B2).

Additionally, in 2009 the Department of Education changed the process and criteria for selection of beneficiaries. Rather than being randomly selected, beneficiary students were now picked by their schools according to their attendance and performance records, as well as their "institutional, cultural and sports commitment" (Alcaldía Mayor de Bogotá 2010). In practice, beneficiary selection is now completely at the school's discretion and the above criteria are not mandatory. For instance, interviewee B25 revealed that the selection conducted by his school considered both the student's financial need and his/her academic performance.

Subsidios also went through institutional change. When it was created back in 2005, the program was placed at the Division of Coverage, which is responsible for policies concerning access to education. However, as the department was restructured in late 2008, a new division was created: the Division of Student Well-Being. *Subsidios* was then transferred to the new division, along with programs such as school feeding, school transportation, and school health. The rationale was that all these programs contribute to enhancing student well-being and, hence, their continuation in school. The scholarship program, however, was transferred to the Division of Secondary and Higher Education, thus becoming institutionally separate from *Subsidios* at the Department of Education. Besides breaking the interdepartment link between the two incentives against high-school dropouts, the restructuring pushed the *Subsidios* program further away from policymaking on education quality. Discussions in the new division mostly concern the allocation of resources and logistical issues, being divorced from pedagogical debates.

5.2   FAMILIAS EN ACCIÓN

In 2009, an agreement was made between Bogota's *Subsidios* program and the national CCT *Familias en Acción*. In order to have the bigger picture of that change it is important to have some minimum understanding of the *"Familias"* program. Details of the program will be skipped, since they could fill pages and pages with information that is very interesting but beyond the scope of this work. As a matter of fact, information on *Familias* is more readily available than on *Subsidios*, since within the international CCT community Colombia is known for the *Familias* program rather than the Bogota program.

Familias was created in 1999 in order to help poor families cope with the effects of the worst financial crisis the country had ever experienced. It was jointly designed by the national government, the World Bank, and the Inter-American Development Bank. According to interviewee B11, the program was modeled after Mexico's *Oportunidades* and Brazil's *Bolsa Escola* (precursor of *Bolsa Familia*). Since then, *Familias* has been continuously funded through international loans, with the World Bank and the IDB taking turns on a yearly basis to provide the necessary funds (interviewee B20).

Familias en Accion was especially designed for rural areas and follows the pattern of making transfers conditional upon children's school attendance. Later, on its implementation, the program also started operating in large urban centers, including Bogota. Initially, its urban population exclusively comprised displaced families that had fled rural areas due to the long-lasting armed conflict between the government, guerillas, and paramilitary groups. Then in 2005 *Acción Social* (social action), the government agency in charge of *Familias*, made the decision to extend the program to urban SISBEN 1 families. In 2009, *Familias* was present in 1100 of Colombia's 1102 municipalities. Its reach jumped from 22,000 families in 1999 – 2 million in 2009 (interviewee B4).

Due to statistics indicating that urban enrollment in primary education was high, cash transfers conditioned upon school attendance were then limited to students enrolled in the 6th–11th grades. That naturally generated some overlap with the *Subsidios* program and heightened the political tension between the local and the national government, which at the time belonged to competing parties.

Despite various political difficulties, there have been attempts to make both programs work in a complementary fashion. *Familias en Accion* was gradually taking over the work with SISBEN 1 families (the poorest), while *Subsidios'* pool of beneficiaries was becoming exclusively comprised of SISBEN 2. One of the reasons for this division of tasks lay in the fact that *Subsidios* benefits were only paid for a maximum of two years, whereas beneficiaries of *Familias* could remain in the program for up to six years (interviewee B2). Also, one of the strings that came attached with the international loans to *Familias* was that it should be exclusively targeted at SISBEN 1 beneficiaries (interviewee B4).

This cooperation between the city and the national government made it possible to expand CCT payments to about 80,000 students/families in 2009 in Bogota. Previously, *Subsidios* had only reached 45,000 students. Naturally, administrative problems amounted when it came to coordinating the two programs and explaining the change to beneficiaries, school principals, and teachers. Misunderstandings mainly arose from the differences between the two programs' features: payment values were slightly different; *Familias* did not have a savings component; and in 2009 *Familias* awarded a bonus payment to 2500 11th graders who graduated from high school[9] (interviewee B7).

In 2012, while a new national law recognized *Familias* as a citizen right (Departamentopara la Prosperidad Social 2013), the program was renamed *MásFamilias en Acción* (More Families in Action). However, it essentially maintained most of its features, as well as its complementary work with the *Subsidios* program in Bogotá.

5.3   *Subsidios* and Education Policies

At the national level, education policies in Colombia had been known for their managerial style and for assigning priority to bringing efficiency to the education system, above all. At the same time, they had counted on remarkable continuity, as the then Uribe administration had maintained Cecilia Maria Velez as the Minister of Education since 2002. For many, that continuity had, in itself, been positive for Colombia's education policies, since in the past, ministers of education did not last in office for longer than a year (interviewee B17).

In the city of Bogota, on the other hand, the past four administrations had put education high on the agenda. As a result, the share of the city's budget assigned to education had continuously grown and reached the impressive mark of 35%. Despite that continuity in terms of the prominence of education in the policy agenda, there was some polarization of opinions in terms of the overall approach that each administration took in education. Many saw the administrations of Samuel Moreno and his predecessor Luis Eduardo Garzón as having "heterodox" approaches to education policy when it came to the idea of the right to education. According to interviewee B24, "two administrations of leftist mayors have 'spoiled' the education sector." This continuity between them was especially due to the fact that they shared the same Secretary of Education, Abel Rodriguez, for most of their terms.

On the other hand, many characterize the preceding administrations of Antanas Mockus and Enrique Peñalosa as attempts to privatize public education in Bogota. This assessment is linked to the fact that they developed a strong policy of building new public schools and giving them in concession to the owners of private schools, who would be responsible for their management. This sort of "charter school" policy still polarizes opinions in the city. Some value the opportunity of having poor kids enjoy the same education quality and school conditions as rich kids. Others find in it a tendency toward privatizing public education (interviewee B5).

One of the hallmarks of the policies adopted by Education Secretary Abel Rodriguez was exactly the expansion and strengthening of programs that were aimed at providing cash or in-kind support to students in lower secondary (*secundaria basica*) and upper secondary education (*educación media*). The administration justified its policy by pointing out that students need to cope with the direct and indirect costs of going to school. When they belong to low-income families with many children, those costs may be unsustainable and students have no other choice but to drop out of school. Thus, it was argued that by providing them with the means to remain in school, the DoE would be assuring their right to education.

The policy not only comprised three "subsidy" programs. It also included the school feeding program, the elimination of school fees, and school busing. Most interviewed school principals and coordinators emphatically championed the provision of school meals in their schools. Interviewee B24 noted that "sometimes the school snack is the only thing that the child eats during the whole day." Some interviewees also highlighted the fact that tuition fees had been abolished up to 6th grade and that the administration's plan was to extend free tuition to the 11th grade, thereby universalizing free education in public schools.

In addition, part of Secretary Rodriguez's policies was the construction of new "mega-schools" and the restoration of existing ones in the districts that suffered the most from scarcity of school seats. As a part of the data collection process for this research, some of those schools were visited. Besides being large schools with the capacity for a large number of students, they had been equipped with technology labs and, in some cases, kitchens for the preparation of hot meals. They were also nice-looking constructions, which seemed to be much appreciated by school personnel and students (interviewee B23).

As previously explained, at the DoE the *Subsidios* program was originally managed by the Division of Coverage, whose mandate was to promote greater school access. By the end of 2008, the department was restructured and a new division was created—the Division for Student Well-Being. In that process, *Subsidios* was transferred to the new division along with other "well-being" programs—school feeding, transportation, and elimination of school fees. If on the one hand the department's restructuring was meant to rationalize program management, on the other hand it had the effect of placing *Subsidios* farther away from the department's divisions that work with education quality.

In reality, there has never been a policy link between *Subsidios* and pedagogical programs. A former DoE official said: "I used to manage the issues related to quality. *Subsidios* was managed by the Sub-Department of Planning" (interviewee B9). That disconnect is reproduced at the school level. According to interviewee B27, "there is no articulation between *Subsidios* and schools' academic work."

Even so, when one looks at the relationship between the *Subsidios* program and the education sector, there is evidence that some level of integration (although not perfect) has been achieved. First, the program is completely owned by the DoE and belongs to the department's core policy agenda, contributing to its policy goal of enhancing "student well-being." Second, schools are immersed in the daily operation of the program, even if only at the administrative level: they are responsible for reporting attendance directly to the program and for selecting beneficiaries. Third, there is a significant amount of debate about the program among education scholars and leaders of teachers unions. Fourth, the program is also known as *"SubsidioEducativo"* (educational subsidy), which makes it clear that Bogota's CCT is truly viewed as an educational program.

5.3.1   Advocacy Coalitions

Three advocacy coalitions have been identified when it comes to education policies in Bogota. The first corresponds to a belief system whose deep core is a functional view of education, one in which schools should be able to educate students to have good grades and become productive workers. Its core belief is that priority should be given to reaching greater efficiency in the public education system. As for its secondary aspects, the preferred policy solutions involve contracting private companies to administer public schools, and providing financial incentives for improved school management. Policymakers in the national Ministry of Education are members of this advocacy coalition. In the words of a leading MoE official, "what the government has been doing is to give more efficiency to the use of resources, of infrastructure, of human resources, so that teachers can be found where children are" (interviewee B17).

The second advocacy coalition represents a belief system whose deep core is the view of education as a fundamental right, rather than a means to achieve an end. Consequently, its core belief is that priority should be assigned to policies that will assure the right to education. Its secondary aspects include policy solutions such as the construction of new schools and programs to help students cope with the direct and indirect costs of education, such as the *Subsidios* program. The administration in charge of Bogota's Department of Education and most interviewed principals and teachers belong to this advocacy coalition.

Third, there is also an advocacy coalition that views education as a complex process, one that is far more than just a means or a right. The following quote better exemplifies it:

> People do not go through an educational process with a single purpose, like acquiring skills that will support individual production and the surrounding environment. The educational process is rather a set of knowledge, abilities, and capacities that go beyond school chairs and involve interpersonal relations, and the generation of ties of authority and respect, resulting in an individual that establishes relationships with the family and the State. (CIDER 2007, p. 2)

As a consequence of such an understanding of the educational process, members of the above advocacy coalition contend that "education subsidies" are deviating policies from the root causes of educational problems. They defend that pedagogical practices should be reformed in order to assure that lessons will be meaningful to students, consequently preventing them from dropping out of school. Scholars, both in education and in other fields are the main representatives of this coalition.

It is interesting to note that the dispute between the "efficiency-based" and the "rights-based" advocacy coalition takes the form of political disputes between competing parties. In other words, the debate can be defined in terms of competing belief systems in education, but also along party lines. And, surprisingly, despite their fundamental ideological differences and political rivalry, both the coalitions have developed their own CCT: *Familias en Accion* in the national/central government and *Subsidios* in the city government. These programs do present some small operational differences, but both work under the same premises.

Curiously, some interviewed members of the "rights-based" coalition and supporters of the city government who were then in office accused the *Familias* program of a lack of transparency, political manipulation, and subjecting families to long queues in order to apply for the program. They considered that *Subsidios* did not present those faulty aspects and that "Bogota has given an example of transparency, very different from what has happened in Familias en Accion" (interviewee B24).

Thus, an analysis of the two powerful advocacy coalitions that dispute the control of educational policies in Colombia has indicated that they do not compete over the continuity or termination of a CCT in Bogota. They do not compete either over the details of the program's operation or the program's link to education quality. Both the coalitions have their own CCT and point the finger to problems in its opponent's program.

Consequently, the Bogota case brings an interesting finding concerning CCTs and education advocacy coalitions: CCTs may fit into different belief systems, be it to the Left or to the Right. And that may eventually help explain part of why CCTs have become diffused across so many countries, no matter what their government's political affiliation is.

Similar to Opportunity NYC, *Subsidios* strengthened the advocacy coalition that dominated education policymaking in the city at the time. Therefore, as it did not work as an external factor for the replacement of the advocacy coalition in office, it could not induce change in policies for educational quality through the mechanism described by Sabatier in his Advocacy Coalition Framework. As reported in the previous section, *Subsidios* is actually very distant from policymaking for improved quality. Although a DoE official said that the selection of students according to their academic performance would improve quality (interviewee B5), it is clear that even if it leads to greater student effort, it is hard to think of how it could change teaching practices, pedagogical methods, and teacher qualifications. Therefore, even though the *Subsidios* program has been owned by the education sector, it has not induced new policies for improved education quality.

5.4   POLITICAL SUSTAINABILITY: PARTY, SCHOOL, AND FAMILY SUPPORT

At the Department of Education, *Subsidios* counted on substantial political will. The following sections analyze *Subsidios'* political sustainability in light of the punctuated equilibrium theory and the civic capacity framework.

5.4.1   *Punctuated-Equilibrium*

Bearing in mind Baumgartner and Jones' punctuated-equilibrium theory, one can argue that the DoE had been able to establish a policy monopoly on how to tackle the dropout issue in Bogota. Throughout various interviews, respondents highlighted the department's policy to counter school dropout and increase graduation rates by enhancing student well-being. The provision of school meals, the payment of "transportation subsidies", of "education subsidies", and school busing were repeatedly mentioned.

According to PET, "policy monopolies have two important characteristics. First, a definable institutional structure is responsible for policymaking, and that structure limits access to the policy process. Second, a powerful supporting idea is associated with the institution" (Baumgartner and Jones 1993, p. 7). Such an institutional structure, also called "policy venue," corresponds to the division of student well-being within Bogota's DoE. As for the powerful idea that backs it up, the division's work has been justified with reference to education as a fundamental right. According to a DoE official, "the functions of the Division of Student Well-Being cluster around children's rights" (interviewee B5). A former official expressed the same viewpoint by affirming that "since 2004 the Department adopted a perspective of guaranteeing the right to education by making sure that this right will not be hindered by the life conditions that affect children" (interviewee B12).

The *Subsidios* program is a part of that policy monopoly and therefore its continuity is assured for as long as the monopoly stands. According to PET, policy change would take place only if a new policy understanding arose with the support of another institutional structure and powerful idea. At least for the moment, there seems to be in Bogota no other prominent understanding of how to best approach school dropout.

As for *Subsidios'* policy image, which is an important element in the framework of a policy monopoly, the majority of interviewees expressed a positive view about the program. Some were more informed about its operational details than others, but in general opinions were positive. Moreover, most had an overall positive assessment about the education policies that have been implemented by the city's last two administrations, indicating that current policies have the potential to remain in place for some time.

5.4.2   Civic Capacity

Among the three cases under study here, *Subsidios* is the one for which this research was better able to assess the presence or absence of civic capacity. This was particularly due to the possibility of speaking to a greater range of actors, especially school personnel.

Principals, teachers, and school coordinators were unanimous in assessing the program as a positive initiative that should be definitely maintained and, if possible, upscaled. Many pointed out that beneficiary students truly need cash transfers due to their family's poor socioeconomic conditions. Some gave examples of how the program has positively impacted students' access to school by allowing them to acquire their own textbooks, pay for transportation, and buy lunch when the school is not yet part of the school feeding program. In the words of interviewee B8, "teachers defend these 'paternalistic' and compensatory projects because they see in them some help to students and to schools."

The new beneficiary selection process—in which schools are in charge of selecting program participants—bolstered support to *Subsidios* among the school community. Some school interviewees declared that they thought it was not fair that in the past good students were not among those who received cash benefits (interviewee B28). The new selection process was expected to correct that unfairness.

As mentioned above, education scholars were particularly critical of cash transfer programs, pointing out that they should only be used as a temporary solution. Scholars strongly emphasized the need for tackling the structural factors that cause educational inequalities in Colombia. Despite that, all the interviewed scholars made a concession for the *Subsidios* program. Interviewee B8, a member of the Colombian academia in education, conceded: "we defend the program transitorily in Bogota but not at the national level, due to the political use that the president's office[10] has made of Familias en Accion. In Bogota there is an interest that is more social than political."

Along these lines, a great number of interviewees expressed a positive opinion about *Subsidios*, but a very critical perspective of *Familias en Accion*. Critics accused the national government of using its CCT for political gain, of not verifying compliance with conditionalities, and of not caring about beneficiaries' dignity by making them stay in line for days to apply for the program.

At the end of the day, no matter what the opinion about CCT programs was, political affiliation or sympathy for the city government (as opposed to the national government) seemed to determine whether there would be support for or opposition to *Subsidios*. At least among those interviewed for this research, no fierce opposition was found.

Besides this study's interviews, the past qualitative evaluation of *Subsidios* had already concluded that parents strongly supported the program. Similar to the opinion expressed by teachers and principals in their interviews, parents would like to see *Subsidios* expanded to a greater number of students (Mayer and Morais de Sa e Silva 2008). Finally, according to CIDER (2007), "the population in general seems to support the program's existence and does not see a perverse incentive in it" (p. 3).

Therefore, as far as civic capacity is concerned, *Subsidios* should not face lack of support for as long as a progressive administration remained in office in the city.

5.5   POLICY BORROWING AND LENDING

5.5.1   Policy Borrowing: Mexico, Brazil

According to interviewees B2 and B6, *Subsidios* was modeled after Mexico's *Oportunidades*[11] and Brazil's *Bolsa Escola* (which at the time had already become *Bolsa Familia*). The program's savings component was specifically inspired by *Jovenes con Oportunidades*,[12] a component of the then *Oportunidades* program. *Jovenes* benefitted adolescents and young adults of *Oportunidades* families who were enrolled in lower and upper secondary school (the last year of *secundaria* and the two years of *bachillerato*). As beneficiaries completed each of these grades, they could accumulate "points" in the program. These points were then turned into cash after the beneficiary completed high school. This strategy was devised to reduce dropout, increase high school completion, and also support enrollment in higher education (Oportunidades 2010).

As for *Bolsa Escola*, it also had a savings component, which was called School Savings (*Poupança Escola*). Yonemura (2005) explains as follows:

> One minimum wage was deposited into a savings account for each child whose family was a beneficiary of the scholarship program if the child successfully completed the grade and was promoted to the next grade. (...) Half of the deposit could be withdrawn if the child reached the 4th grade or the 8th grade, depending on when they started the program. The balance could be withdrawn only when the student completed high school. (p. 52)

The borrowing from Mexico and Brazil can be explained as a consequence of the economics of policy borrowing (Steiner-Khamsi, 2004). According to the borrowing and lending literature, one of the reasons that governments borrow policy models from abroad is to please donors in order to access funding. In the case of Bogota, the city government wanted to obtain an external loan, especially from the Inter-American Development Bank. Since both *Oportunidades* and *Bolsa Escola/Bolsa Familia* are favorites among the international community of donors, reference to these programs could facilitate the approval of funds. Thus, policy borrowing was not a result of external pressure, but rather a mechanism to impress donors.

Although *Oportunidades* and *Bolsa Escola/Bolsa Familia* were used as models in the design of the *Subsidios* program, the latter was not created as an exact copy of the two programs. The direct involvement of school personnel in its operation, the comparison of three different payment schemes, and the signature on the "terms of commitment" by participating families are among its peculiar features. Program designers had room for innovation and that may be associated with the fact that among them were US-based researchers who pushed for the making of *Subsidios* a new experiment.

5.5.2   Policy Lending: Not Internationally Prominent

For both the IDB and the involved US-based researchers, *Subsidios* was purposefully designed and evaluated to inform other countries about the effectiveness of different payment schemes. Although the program has operated for years, it has not been present in most CCT studies and, when it is, it is often portrayed as an experiment (Barrera-Osorio et al. 2008; Fiszbein and Schady 2009).

However, little has been done to promote *Subsidios* in other countries. This could be due to no media coverage outside of Colombia; of the four articles that have been published on the program, none was featured in a foreign newspaper. Additionally, if one searches the World Bank's and the IDB's website for *Subsidios Condicionados a la Asistencia Escolar*, the search results in only 3 pages in the former and 6 in the latter. Compared with the other two case studies analyzed here, the results are, respectively, 1210 and 83 pages for *Bolsa Familia*, and 96 and 1 for Opportunity NYC.

According to an IDB representative, *Subsidios'* international "low-profile" derives from the absence of efforts by the Department of Education to give international exposure to the program (interviewee B21). However, neither the World Bank nor the IDB have included *Subsidios* in international exchanges such as visits by foreign delegations or the frequent videoconferences with representatives of CCT programs in Latin America (in which managers of *Familias en Accion* are the ones invited to participate).

The reason behind the banks' lack of efforts to export *Subsidios* may be related to some "reverse" politics of policy lending. As in the case of policy borrowing, the borrowing and lending theory argues that policy lending occurs when a policy is in need of legitimization at home. The export of that policy is used as a sign of its value, as a certification strategy. In that case, political factors contribute to the promotion of policy lending (Steiner-Khamsi 2004). In contrast, "reverse" politics would mean that politics work as a constraint to policy lending. In Bogota, political disputes between the national government and the city government led to the prevalence of *Familias en Accion* in the international arena. Both the IDB and the World Bank, as providers of large yearly loans to finance *Familias*, could not "upset" the national government by internationally promoting the CCT implemented by its political opponent. Consequently, there were minimal efforts to promote the *Subsidios* model and experience outside of Colombia.

Interestingly, inside Colombia some policy lending did take place between *Subsidios* and *Familias en Accion*. *Familias* added a new element to its operation in urban centers: high-school students are awarded a bonus payment when they graduate. According to interviewee B1, this new element was a result of policy learning from *Subsidios'* first evaluation results, that is, the finding that modality 3 had the greatest impact upon attendance, enrollment, and graduation rates among participants. Naturally, the national government did not officially acknowledge that it had borrowed ideas from its competing CCT.

Notes

1. SISBEN stands for System for the Identification of Potential Beneficiaries of Social Programs. It is a unified measurement system of citizens' standard of living. It classifies them into six different strata. The lower the

family score in the system, the poorer it is and the more eligible for participation in social programs.

2. See a description of Jovenes con Oportunidades in the 'Policy Borrowing' section of this chapter.

3. The program's name has been translated as Conditional Subsidies for School Attendance (Barrera-Osorio et al. 2008).

4. The exchange rate between the US dollar and the Colombian peso was around 1:2000 at the time.

5. The public education system in Colombia is comprised of three cycles: 1st to 5th (basic primary education), 6th to 8th (basic secondary education), and 9th to 11th (mid secondary education).

6. Programs were at the postsecondary level but were not equivalent to college degrees. They generally involved six semesters of study in careers such as tourism, accounting, and communication technology. Education-related and health-related programs were not included.

7. In order to enroll Subsidios participants and receive tuition payments from the Department of Education, private postsecondary schools had to receive accreditation from Bogota's DoE. During the program's first year, all private schools that were members of FODESEP (Fondo de Desarrollo de la Educación Superior/Higher Education Development Fund) were eligible to enroll program beneficiaries.

8. Different from Bolsa Familia, Subsidios beneficiaries are not entitled to payments during vacation months. They are only eligible for 5 payments throughout the ten months of classes.

9. The bonus payment was not announced in advance and therefore cannot be considered an additional incentive for graduation as in Subsidios' former modality 3.

10. Reference to the administration to then President Uribe.

11. Now called *Prospera*.

12. Now called *Becas Prospera*.

REFERENCES

Alcaldía Mayor de Bogotá. (2010). *Subsidio Educativo Condicionado a la Asistencia Escolar.* Retrieved January 29, 2010, from http://www.bogota.gov.co/portel/libreria/php/frame_detalle_scv.php?h_id=23206.

Barrera-Osorio, F., Bertrand, M., Linden, L., & Perez-Calle, F. (2008). *Conditional cash transfers in education: Design features, peer and sibling effects. Evidence from a randomized experiment in Colombia.* Retrieved November 15, 2008, from http://web.worldbank.org/WBSITE/EXTERNAL/TOPICS/EXTEDUCATION/0,,contentMDK:21631004~isCURL:Y~menuPK:2448393~pagePK:210058~piPK:210062~theSitePK:282386,00.html.

Baumgartner, F., & Jones, B. (1993). *Agendas and instability in American politics*. Chicago: University of Chicago Press.

CIDER. (2007). *Relatoría del debate sobre educación en Bogotá D.C.* [Report on the debate about education in Bogotá D.C.]. Retrieved January 29, 2010, from http://jatorres.uniandes.edu.co/Documentos/Relatorias%20 Seminario%20Jaime/Relatoría%20EDUCACIÓN%20-%20Seminario%20 Maestria%20CIDER%20(jul%2007).pdf.

Departamentopara la Prosperidad Social. (2013). *Rediseño del Programa Familias en Accion* (DocumentoOperativoTecnico No. 1). Retrieved October 28, 2016, from http://www.prosperidadsocial.gov.co/inf/doc/Documentos%20 compartidos/Documento%20Operativo%20Técnico%201%20-%20 Rediseño%20del%20programa%20Más%20Familias%20en%20Acción.PDF.

Fiszbein, A., & Schady, N. (2009). *Conditional cash transfers: Reducing present and future poverty*. Washington, DC: The World Bank Group.

IDB. (2005). *Documento conceptual de proyecto*. Programa de Equidad en Educacion en Bogota. Retrieved November 15, 2008, from http://idbdocs. iadb.org/wsdocs/getdocument.aspx?docnum=571342.

IDB. (2006). *Bogota equity in education program*. Retrieved March 2, 2008, from http://www.iadb.org/projects/Project.cfm?project=CO-L1010&Language= English.

Mayer, P., & Morais de Sa e Silva, M. (2008). *Bogotá Equity in Education: Conditional subsidies for school attendance and postsecondary study. A qualitative evaluation*. Unpublished manuscript.

Oportunidades. (2010). *Jovenes con Oportunidades*. Retrieved January 26, 2010, from http://www.oportunidades.gob.mx/jovenes/jovenes.html.

Secretaria de Educación del Distrito Capital. (2010). *Subsidio de Transporte* [Transportation subsidy]. Retrieved February 2, 2010, from http://matricu-labdl.redp.edu.co/sistemat02/sed/websubsidios/transporte/compromisos. htm.

Steiner-Khamsi, G. (2004). *The politics of educational borrowing and lending*. New York: Teachers College Press.

World Bank. (2006). *Conditional cash transfers*. Retrieved October 15, 2008, from http://web.worldbank.org/WBSITE/EXTERNAL/TOPICS/EXTSOCIAL PROTECTION/EXTSAFETYNETSANDTRANSFERS/0,,contentMDK:2061 5138~menuPK:282766~pagePK:148956~piPK:216618~theSitePK:282761,00. html.

CHAPTER 6

The Largest Conditional Cash Transfer in the World

Bolsa Família, the Brazilian national conditional cash transfer (CCT), reaches 14 million families or 47.1 million people (Paiva et al. 2016). Its scale is off the charts and its program management is quite intricate. Despite its significant scope, *Bolsa Família* involves a budget of only 0.5% of the Brazilian Gross Domestic Product (GDP) (World Bank 2010). In 2015, it paid over 7 billion US dollars[1] in cash transfers to beneficiary families. From 2004 to 2011, 22,168,469 persons were raised above the extreme poverty line as a result of the program implementation.

The program is centrally managed by the Ministry of Social Development and Fight Against Hunger (MDS),[2] specifically by its National Department of Citizen's Income (SENARC). As a federation, Brazil has decentralized social assistance, education, and health services to the state and municipal levels. Consequently, *Bolsa Família* depends on the coordination between different line-ministries and also on the cooperation between different levels of government. This multi-institutional operation will be later presented in detail.

Bolsa Família has been extensively documented both in Brazil and abroad. Among the three cases under study here, it is certainly the one with the largest number of studies and evaluations. The most complete works on the program include Britto (2004), Lindert et al. (2007), Bastagli (2008), Cotta (2009), and Campello, et al. (2014). These works provide a complete account of *Bolsa Família*'s initial development, operational features, and modifications with time.

© The Author(s) 2017
M. Morais de Sá e Silva, *Poverty Reduction, Education, and the Global Diffusion of Conditional Cash Transfers*, DOI 10.1007/978-3-319-53094-9_6

Table 6.1   CCTs in Brazil (1995–2016)

Program	Scope	Party
1st Bolsa Escola Guarantee of Minimum Family Income	Federal District Campinas	Workers' Party (PT) Brazilian Social Democratic Party (PSDB)
2nd Various local CCTs	State and municipal	Various
3rd Federal Guarantee of Minimum Family Income	National, but targeted to priority municipalities	PSDB
4th Federal Bolsa Escola	National, reaching virtually all Brazilian municipalities	PSDB
5th Bolsa Familia (2003–2016)	National, reaching all municipalities and an increasingly larger group of beneficiaries. In 2011, the program becomes part of the larger poverty-reduction strategy Brasil sem Miséria (Brazil without Extreme Poverty).	PT

Different from Opportunity NYC and Subsidios, *Bolsa Familia* was preceded by local, smaller CCTs. As presented in Chap. 1, the programs *Bolsa Escola* and Guarantee of Minimum Family Income were the precursors to *Bolsa Familia* and were among the first CCTs to be ever created way back in the 1990s. Whereas they first emerged as local initiatives, in 2001 the Brazilian federal government launched a Federal *Bolsa Escola*, still during the administration of the former President Fernando Henrique Cardoso. It was only in 2003/2004, with the beginning of the Lula administration, that *Bolsa Familia* was created out of the merge and expansion of Federal *Bolsa Escola* with two other federal programs— *Bolsa Alimentação* (food grant) and *Vale Gás* (cooking gas voucher).

For easy visualization of the initial sequence of CCT programs in Brazil, Table 6.1 was prepared.

6.1   *Bolsa Familia*'s Early Days

With the end of the Cardoso administration and the victory of Luis Inacio Lula da Silva and his Workers' Party in the 2002 elections, a period of transition began for CCTs in Brazil. Initially, the Federal *Bolsa Escola* was maintained, especially since its greatest advocate, Cristovam

Buarque, had been elected Senator and was then appointed the new Minister of Education.

In the field of poverty reduction, President Lula had strongly based his campaign on the promise that he would end starvation and guarantee that every Brazilian would have access to at least three meals a day. That promise was turned into the immediate creation of the *Fome Zero* (zero hunger) Program. In order to house the program a new ministry was created—the Special Ministry of Food Security and Fight Against Hunger (MESA).

More than a federal program, Zero Hunger was planned as a macropolicy that would involve both short-term and long-term strategies. In 2003, MESA strived to put together a number of subprograms that would jointly comprise Zero Hunger; one of them was *Cartão Alimentação* (Food Card), a CCT focused on improving food security for the poor.

Nonetheless, the implementation of Zero Hunger did not come easily. As time went by its results were not clear, various implementation issues arose, and criticisms started to abound. With that came the discussion of whether Brazil's main problem was that of hunger or, beyond that, a broader poverty issue (interviewee C2).

The World Bank got into this discussion by preparing a number of policy notes on social protection. Their papers gathered evidence on food-based versus cash-based transfers, and on targeted versus universalized policies (interviewee C2). As a whole, through these papers the bank advocated for the adoption of the CCT model, as opposed to creating a new strategy of social policy through Zero Hunger.

In order to convince the new administration, a high-level meeting was held in March 2003 gathering President Lula, World Bank President James Wolfensohn, and the Senior World Bank Economist for Latin America. The bank also brought to the meeting Santiago Levy, Mexico's key figure in the creation of *Progresa/Oportunidades*. Levy gave a testimony about his experience and advised Lula to shift his social strategy, building upon existing CCTs and unifying them (interviewee C6). According to Lindert et al. (2007):

> Subsequent to that meeting, President Lula formally requested that officials in the (former) Ministry of Social Assistance prepare a proposal for an integrated program. A group of representatives of the Government and Brazilian institutes worked – with technical assistance from the World Bank and other donors – to explore options for the various design parameters for such a program. (pp. 13–14)

The bank's advice resonated with discussions and studies that were already underway in Brazil. Researchers at IPEA (*Instituto de Pesquisas Econômicas Aplicadas*/Institute of Applied Economic Research) had been questioning what to do with the *Cadastro Único* (Single Registry), a database created to consolidate beneficiary information about all federal social programs. As part of that discussion, they started analyzing different programs and came to the conclusion that the existing federal CCTs were the best social programs in place. The federal government was simultaneously implementing four conditional cash transfer programs at the time: (1) *Bolsa Escola*, which was housed at the Ministry of Education; (2) *Auxílio Gás*, a CCT that supported the purchase of cooking gas; (3) *Bolsa Alimentação* (food grant), which was based at the Ministry of Health; and (4) thenewly created *Cartão Alimentação* (food card), which was part of the Zero Hunger initiative. IPEA researchers then ran various simulations and concluded that the best option was to streamline and strengthen those CCTs (interviewee C2). Their unification was expected to generate gains in efficiency and policy coherence.

That proposal met resistance from other groups of experts and government officials involved in social policymaking. Resistance especially came from the heads of Zero Hunger, who could foresee that the proposal to merge all the four CCTs would create a mega social program that would take the spotlight away from Zero Hunger. Opposition was also presented by those ahead of individual CCTs, like Cristovam Buarque. He argued that the unification of programs would make the monitoring of school attendance more difficult. Naturally, he was also against moving the program away from the Ministry of Education (interviewee C15). Despite these arguments and opposition, Lula made the decision to merge the three CCTs inherited from the previous administration and Zero Hunger's *Cartão Alimentação*. It was out of this merger that *Bolsa Família* was created.

The *Bolsa Família* Program was formally created by Provisional Measure[3] 132 of 20 October 2003. The measure was later turned into Law 10.836 of 09 January 2004. At first the program was housed at the *Bolsa Familia* Department, which was directly under the President's office. In early 2004, it was transferred to the newly created Ministry of Social Development and Fight Against Hunger (MDS).

MDS was the end product of another merger. It resulted from the institutional unification between the Ministry of Social Assistance, the Special Ministry of Food Security and Fight Against Hunger (MESA), and the *Bolsa Familia* Department. During its 12 years of existence (2004–2016), MDS had a structure that mirrored its preceding institutions. It was comprised, among others, by the National Department of Social Assistance, the National Department of Food Security, and the National Department of Citizen's Income (to which *Bolsa Familia* belongs). From then on, the Ministry of Education lost oversight over *Bolsa Escola's* beneficiaries and became responsible for assisting MDS in obtaining attendance records of *Bolsa Familia's* beneficiary students. According to the law that created *Bolsa Familia* (Law 10.836/2004):

> At the federal level it is the responsibility of the Ministry of Health and of the Ministry of Education to regulate the conditionalities that correspond to them and to verify their fulfillment by families; to monitor and solve deficiencies in service supply by federated units[4]; to follow up on the evolution of social indicators; to coordinate with local councils about program implementation; to participate in decisions concerning the centralized functions of program management. (registry, payment of benefits, monitoring and evaluation)

During the *Bolsa Escola* years, UN agencies and multilateral banks demonstrated support for Brazil's CCT efforts, as mentioned above. After the creation of *Bolsa Familia*, support remained unabated. Hall (2008) reported that:

> A few months later in June 2004, the World Bank approved a US$ 572 million sector-wide loan to support Bolsa Familia. It provides funding for cash transfers (96 per cent) as well as technical assistance to develop a unified database, improve targeting, develop a system for monitoring and evaluation and strengthen institutional capacity within MDS (World Bank 2004). Later that year, the Inter-American Development Bank (IDB) approved a loan of US$ 1 billion for the program, with a promise of up to twice this amount depending on progress. (p. 806)

6.2   *Bolsa Familia's* Features

Similar to the former *Bolsa Escola*, *Bolsa Familia* transfers a certain amount of cash to the female head of the household provided that children are enrolled in school and demonstrate a minimum school attendance of 85% if they are 6–15 years old. If the beneficiary children are 16 or 17 years old, a minimum of 75% of school attendance is required.

Additionally, the program encompasses health-related conditionalities, such as the due immunization of children younger than 6 years old, prenatal checkups, and medical follow-up of nursing mothers (MDS 2008). The program has gone through a number of adjustments and payment amounts have also changed, especially since the creation of the "Brazil without Extreme Poverty Plan," of which *Bolsa Família* is a part. In 2016, *Bolsa Família*'s monthly payment values were as follows:

1. A basic transfer of 85 reais (about US$25[5]) to extremely poor families, defined as families with a monthly per capita income of less than 85 reais.[6]
2. For families with a monthly per capita income of up to 170 reais (US$51), variable transfers[7] of 39 reais (US$13) for each child up to 15 years old and/or pregnant or nursing woman in the household. In the case of child benefits, a record of a minimum of 85% of school attendance is required. A maximum of only five of those transfers are paid to each household (maximum of 195 reais or US$60).
3. Also, for families with a monthly per capita income of up to 170 reais, a variable transfer of 46 reais (US$14) per adolescent aged 16 or 17 years old, up to the maximum of two adolescents. A minimum of 75% of school attendance is required, although failure to comply with this condition only leads to loss of this specific transfer amount, rather than of the whole transfer as in the case of children up to 15 years old.
4. In the case of families whose monthly per capita income falls below the extreme poverty line of 85 reais even after receiving *Bolsa Família*'s transfers, there is the "Benefit to Overcome Extreme Poverty" (Hellman 2015). This transfer amount is calculated specifically for each family and is aimed at making sure that the family's final income will rise above the extreme poverty line. This transfer modality is relatively new and was introduced with the creation of the Brazil without Extreme Poverty Plan.

Hence, except for families receiving the Benefit to Overcome Extreme Poverty, the total transfer amount varies from 39 reais (US$13) for a poor family with only one child to 372 reais[8] (around US$124) for an extremely poor family with three children and two 16/17-year-old adolescents. For easy reference, the Brazilian monthly minimum wage is currently set at 880 reais, which roughly corresponds to US$290.

As Brazil does not have an official poverty line, eligibility thresholds and transfer amounts were originally based on those of the four CCTs that originated *Bolsa Familia*. The idea was not to produce loss of benefits as participants were transferred across programs (Lindert et al. 2007). Since 2004, transfer amounts and income reference values have been updated by Presidential decisions. They are justified on the basis of annual rises in the official minimum wage and in national inflation indices, but are not indexed to them. In other words, the President has discretionary power to alter program values.

Bolsa Familia started off with 3.8 million families in December 2003 (Lindert et al. 2007). From there the pool of beneficiaries was expanded by incorporating families from the preceding four CCTs and through the registration of new families. From 2004 to 2006 the program was rapidly scaledup, reaching 11.1 million families in 2006. This figure corresponded to estimates of the total number of families whose per capita income was below the estimated poverty line. In 2009, MDS decided to expand the number of beneficiaries to 12.4 million families, arguing that the intention was to include families with vulnerable incomes, the so-called transitional poor. In 2010 the program was further expanded, reaching 12.9 million families. With the creation of the Brazil without Extreme Poverty Plan, the mark of close to 14 million families was reached.

6.3   Implementation of a Large-Scale CCT

Bolsa Familia is such a massive program that its numbers are overwhelming. In terms of education, it benefits 17 million students, which corresponds to 30% of the entire student population in Brazilian public schools (interviewee C12). It reaches each and every Brazilian municipality, totalling 5570. Not the least, *Bolsa Familia* involves a budget corresponding to 0.5% of the country's total GDP (Hellman 2015).

At first sight, *Bolsa Familia*'s scale would not encourage comparison with other programs, especially small, local CCTs such as *Subsidios* and Opportunity NYC. However, for the questions being explored in this book, it will be important to look at a large-scale CCTs and take into account the additional variables that are introduced by scaling-up.

One of the main challenges of operating such a large CCT is making sure that the program is duly implemented at the local level. Brazil is a federation comprised by federal, state, and municipal governments; there is no hierarchy among them and their division of responsibilities is defined by the 1988 Constitution.

In education, for instance, service provision is the direct responsibility of states and municipalities, except for higher education. The federal government, through the Ministry of Education, is responsible for "coordinating the national education policy, linking the different government levels and education systems, and playing a normative, redistributive, and complementary role in relation to the other educational institutions" (Brazil 1996). As the federal government is often in the privileged position of controlling funds that are not tied to current expenses, it is able to create and finance programs of a national scope such as *Bolsa Família*.

At the local level, families can only benefit from *Bolsa Família* if the municipal government agrees to collaborate with program implementation by signing the "Terms of Adherence." That document specifies the set of local responsibilities, including: to verify family documents and enter family information on the Single Registry[9] database; to assign a local focal point to the program; to monitor and report on beneficiary compliance with conditionalities; to update family information on the Single Registry at least once every two years; and to create a municipal council comprised by government and civil society representatives to oversee program implementation (Lindert et al. 2007). Despite all these requirements, every municipal government in the country has agreed to participate in *Bolsa Família*. Not a single mayor has opted out of the program, which may be considered as an indication of its political strength, as discussed further below.

Municipalities are required to register every family with a monthly per capita income of less than 170 reais in the *CadastroÚnico*database. Nonetheless, registration does not guarantee that a family will participate in *Bolsa Família*. This is because each municipality has a quota of program participation. Quotas have been calculated by the Brazilian Institute of Geography and Statistics (IBGE) on the basis of estimations of families in poverty in each municipality.

Although registration in the Single Registry is done at the local level, the final selection of *Bolsa Família*'s participating families is centralized and automatically carried out by the National Department of Citizen's

Income (SENARC) and Caixa, the Brazilian federal public bank. This process is done through a software that makes use of algorithms for random selection. Thus, there is limited room for political manipulation of the program at the local or central levels, as local managers or political leaders cannot guarantee to families whether and when they would be accepted into the program.

In order to encourage dedication to *Bolsa Familia*'s management by municipal governments, MDS created the Index of Decentralized Management (*Índice de Gestão Descentralizada*—IGD 2010a). It is a composite index of four measures: the Single Registry coverage rate[10]; the rate of updates in the Single Registry; the percentage of families whose children have their school attendance duly monitored; and the percentage of families for which there is information on compliance with health conditionalities. The municipal IGD[11] is the resulting means of these four measures.

Besides bringing transparency to *Bolsa Familia*'s local management and making local governments accountable, the index is also used as a basis for defining how much financial support the federal government should provide to municipal governments to compensate them for part of the costs they incur with the management of *Bolsa Familia*. MDS has developed a formula according to which the amount of funds to be transferred depends on the municipal IGD, as well as on the local number of *Bolsa Familia* participants. The formula is as follows (MDS 2010a):

[IGD × R\$ 2.50 × (number of beneficiary families + 200)]

If municipalities do not meet a minimum IGD threshold (0.55), they are not entitled to any transfer (MDS 2010b). In 2010, for instance, MDS transferred a total amount of 22.5 million Reais to 5422 municipalities in Brazil (MDS 2010b).

6.4   EDUCATION CONDITIONALITIES

Compared to the other two programs under analysis in this study, *Bolsa Familia* is the least demanding when it comes to the set of education-related requirements. Simply, the family shall demonstrate that all children are duly enrolled in school at the time it applies for the program through the Single Registry. Once the family is randomly selected, it receives an information package, along with the ATM card issued in the name of the female head of the household.[12] The package explains

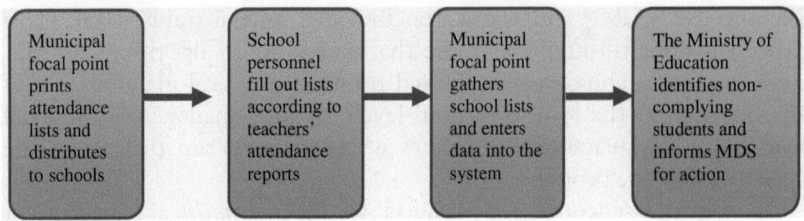

Fig. 6.1   Information flow in the school attendance monitoring system

that, besides health-related conditionalities, 6–15 year-old children need to attend a minimum of 85% of classes and 16 to 17-year-old adolescents attend a minimum of 75% of school days.

However, simple as this may seem, this is a complicated enterprise when it comes to checking whether 17 million students, scattered across thousands of municipalities, have duly fulfilled the requirements. To make it more complicated, the government is also interested in getting to know the reasons for student absenteeism when it occurs.

Monitoring of conditionality compliance has been an issue throughout the history of *Bolsa Familia*. During the program's first year of operation—2004—conditionalities were not monitored due to the transition from previous programs. Since then, every time there is some indication that the government has not followed up on conditionalities the media readily denounces the problem. Health conditionalities are still an issue, but in education there has been considerable progress. The Ministry of Education[13] has created and continuously improved an intricate national system of school attendance monitoring for *Bolsa Familia* beneficiaries (Fig. 6.1).

The system, which is a part of *Projeto Presença* (attendance project), is based on a network of municipal focal points. Each municipal Department of Education designates a focal point who formally agrees to be held accountable for the monthly reporting of school attendance records of every *Bolsa Familia* student in the municipality.[14] The first task of the municipal focal point is to print attendance lists containing the names and information about *Bolsa Familia* students enrolled in each school. The lists are then handed to the school personnel, which fills them out by reporting the number and reason for individual absences. This procedure is to be carried out by principals and their teams, and not by teachers, so as to avoid that they may want to protect or punish students by incorrectly reporting class attendance. In other words, teachers report daily attendance for the whole class, not knowing which students are *Bolsa Familia* beneficiaries. School principals or their delegates then transcribe beneficiaries' absences to the program's list. Finally, focal points at the DoE gather all the school lists and enter data into an online database (interviewee C12).

The school attendance monitoring system connects 22,000 users, who monthly report class attendance for 17 million students enrolled in 168,000 public schools (Escola Nacional de Administração Pública 2010). In 2016, 91.8% of student beneficiaries had their school attendance duly registered by the program (MDSA 2016a).

Through the years, the MoE has continuously worked on making system improvements so as to increase monitoring percentages. The ministry has also strived to improve the quality of the information gathered. Earlier it was common to find municipalities that would report 100% of class attendance for all *Bolsa Familia* beneficiaries. As the ministry succeeded in creating awareness about the importance of duly reporting class attendance, the challenge now was how to obtain accurate information on the reasons why individual students missed classes. Until recently, the majority of municipalities would report that the reason was unknown (interviewee C12).

In New York, noncompletion of an incentivized activity by definition meant that students and their families would not receive the corresponding money transfer. In Bogota, students who did not reach the minimum class attendance requirements did not receive the transfer for the corresponding two-month period. Nor did they receive the end-of-year bonus if they did not finish the school year. In Brazil, however, as soon as a family is selected for the program, it receives a first payment. Conditionality compliance is only checked post-payment. Additionally, the consequences of noncompliance are gradual and involve a series of steps. The sequence of measures that follow noncompliance is detailed in MDS (2010c), which has informed the preparation of Table 6.2.

This gradual sequence of measures is consonant with *Bolsa Familia*'s overall approach to conditionalities. Rather than viewing them as incentives or rewards for new behavior (Opportunity NYC) or as a contribution to student well-being (Subsidios), *Bolsa Familia* approaches conditionalities as a means for the realization of social rights. Failure to comply with conditionalities is viewed as a "red flag" (Lindert et al. 2007), indicating that the family may be in a situation of vulnerability

Table 6.2 Measures taken after noncompliance With *Bolsa Familia's* conditionalities

Noncompliance	Measure
First	A warning note is mailed to the family. The note informs that the family has failed to fulfill program requirements and explains the potential consequences in the case of continued noncompliance
Second	The transfer is suspended for 30 days. However, the family may recover the suspended transfer in the following payment cycle if it resumes compliance
Third	Transfers are suspended for 60 days. However, the family may recover the suspended transfers in the following payment cycle if it resumes compliance
Fourth	Transfers are suspended for 60 days. The family will not be able to recover the payments
Fifth	Family participation in *Bolsa Familia* may be cancelled

and in need of further governmental support. Local governments are advised to follow-up on the situation of noncompliant families and to support them in getting back on track in the program.

6.5   *Bolsa Familia* and Education Policies

Among all the interviewees for this case, there was consensus that *Bolsa Familia* is not an education policy. Interviewee C11 explicitly said that:

> This kind of program works as an income policy, as a policy for income redistribution. It is not a policy that is jointly designed by the actors who are responsible for education (…) The idea that the *Bolsa* policy is educational policy is completely false.

Additionally, a high-level official at the Ministry of Education explained that the ministry's role in *Bolsa Familia* "was to structure the program to assess compliance with conditionalities and establish the flow of information to the Ministry that makes the transfers so that it can suspend or cancel benefits in the cases of noncompliance with program requirements." Thus, the MoE does not play any further role in the design and implementation of *Bolsa Familia* beyond issues of education conditionalities.

When asked about the contribution of *Bolsa Familia* to promoting the ministry's policy objectives, official C16 responded that the program is viewed in education as a *"Bolsa Permanência"* (grant/stipend to remain in school). It helps families maintain their children in school and therefore is a part of the set of programs that the government has created to support public school students, such as the national school feeding program, the program of free textbooks, and school busing for rural students. "These programs, along with Bolsa Família, create an environment of sustainability for children to have access to school and remain enrolled" (interviewee C16). Hence, *Bolsa Familia* is not expected to be linked to quality aspects of education at the federal policymaking level.

Two interviewed scholars revealed that the limited connection between *Bolsa Familia* and education is also manifest in Brazilian academia. Interviewee C8 said that there are only scattered works on *Bolsa Familia* authored by education scholars in Brazil. According to him, cash transfers are not a priority in the education research agenda, which are predominantly studied by economists (interviewee C8). When asked about the reason why education researchers have been absent from *Bolsa Familia* debates, scholar C11 attributed the reason to the mismatch between the nature of educational research in Brazil and the kind of research that is usually developed around CCTs. According to the scholar, education academia in Brazil is predominantly dedicated to philosophical works, quantitative research being still incipient. Consequently, economists and other researchers with quantitative skills are the ones who have carried out studies and evaluations of *Bolsa Familia* (interviewee C11).

The school community is even at a greater distance from *Bolsa Familia*'s design and daily operations. Except for the reporting of eventual absences of beneficiary students, schools have not played any role in terms of debating *Bolsa Familia*, helping strengthen the program, or improving its impact by working on the quality of instruction that beneficiaries receive. The quality debate has existed for a long time in the country, but has not strengthened or changed since *Bolsa Familia* was introduced. Besides the divorce between education and *Bolsa Familia* at the policymaking level, the limited involvement of schools in policy decisions in Brazil has also contributed to the existing reality. According to (Draibe 2003, cited in Yonemura 2005, p. 29):

> Brazil did not have a tradition of active involvement of school communities or associations in policymaking. Although adequate legal provisions did exist, associations such as parent-teacher associations, school councils and

municipal councils of education were not involved in the implementation of education policy until the mid-1990s. Another political challenge was that since the 1970s the middle class had left the public school system and migrated to private schools. These phenomena explained the reason why beneficiary groups in the public school system lacked the outspoken actors to represent them and to advocate for their benefit.

When asked about the educational advantages and disadvantages brought by the unification of CCTs and the consequent end of *Bolsa Escola*, some interviewees gave some interesting answers. A high level official at the Ministry of Education emphasized that the unification of programs and the scaling-up of *Bolsa Familia* allowed for the expansion of school attendance conditionalities from 5 to 17 million students (interviewee C16). For him, this is a gain because conditionalities have led to increased enrolment and attendance. Although parents are mandated by law to send their kids to school, it has been impossible to enforce that law with all families. Consequently, education conditionalities end up being more efficient in getting children to school.

On the other hand, interviewee C15 regrets that the name *escola* (school) was dropped from the program's title, arguing that it weakened the idea that the transfer is meant to allow families to keep their children in school. According to him, under *Bolsa Escola* families viewed the transfer as a "salary" that was paid to them because they kept their children in school. Under *Bolsa Familia*, the interviewee argues, families rather consider that they receive a "handout" because they are poor (interviewee C15).

These divergences aside, the fact is that the policy link between *Bolsa Familia* and education is not too obvious, being limited to the program's conditionalities of school enrollment and attendance. Interviewed government officials and researchers, however, indicated that that was exactly the contribution expected from *Bolsa Familia* in terms of education. The fundamental premise is that poor children are not in school because their families lack the means to do so. In the words of interviewee C16, "sometimes poor children do not attend school because they do not have basic items such as the school uniform." Hence, the program is simply expected to provide poor families with the financial means to enroll their children in school and to make sure that they attend classes on a regular basis. It is expected to lead to greater access, but quality is not seen as an issue to be dealt with by the program.

That being *Bolsa Familia*'s sole mission in education, the few existing evaluations have indicated that the program has had positive impacts. De la Briere et al. (2007) reviewed all available evaluations of conditional cash transfers in Brazil at the time—not only of *Bolsa Familia*, but of its predecessors as well. They report evidence indicating that Brazilian CCTs have contributed to increasing school enrollment and attendance and to reducing dropout among beneficiary students. On the other hand, it was also found that grade repetition rates had slightly increased. That was, however, an expected finding, since the program brings into schools students who are more likely to have a poor educational background and who are expected to have greater difficulties progressing through school (interviewee C3).

In another study, Glewwe and Kassouf (2008) developed a model to assess *Bolsa Escola*'s and *Bolsa Familia*'s joint impacts on enrollment, dropout, and grade promotion. They used data from MoE's yearly school census covering all grades from the first to the eighth. For them, there was consistent increase in enrollment and grade promotion for all grades, as well as reduction in dropout rates across all years of primary education.

Beyond the numbers, an MDS official argued that *Bolsa Familia* has also given a positive contribution to bringing back to public schools children who are often "evicted" from the school system (interviewee C18). These are often children from vulnerable families, with weak educational backgrounds, greater learning difficulties, nutritional deficiencies, and sometimes chronic diseases. They are more likely to miss classes, fail the school year, and drop out of school. As they give up, schools do not follow-up on them and do not systematically take the effort to bring them back. *Bolsa Familia*, however, has forced a change in this situation through the conditions related to school enrollment and attendance. Besides, MDS hopes that each municipal Department of Education will work directly with individual families in tackling the reasons for their children's absenteeism and dropout (interviewee C18). Again, *Bolsa Familia*'s greatest role in education has been granting greater school access for the poor.

Nonetheless, there is still skepticism about *Bolsa Familia*'s real impact in terms of human capital accumulation due to the poor quality of schools (*The Economist* 2007; interviewee C11). World Bank specialists have voiced concern about the quality of Brazilian public schools and how that limits *Bolsa Familia*'s potential impact on human capital (interviewees C2 and C4). In that regard, De la Briere et al. (2007) state that:

CCT beneficiary children do not obtain better learning outcomes than their non-beneficiary counterparts. Clearly, CCTs need to be complemented by investments in improving the quality of Brazil's education system to help reduce repetition and improve learning outcomes. (p. 32)

Despite the awareness that beneficiaries' schools are deficient in quality, *Bolsa Familia* managers have not set the goal of working with the Ministry of Education in order to create new policies for improved quality. On the one hand it is argued that quality efforts cannot be exclusively targeted at *Bolsa Familia* beneficiaries; being a problem that affects the entire student population in public schools, it is beyond the scope of the program's mission. The following section on advocacy coalitions reinforces this finding.

6.6   ADVOCACY COALITIONS

In education, at least three advocacy coalitions have been identified in Brazil. The first, represented by the federal administration during the Workers' Party years (2003–2016), used to have in its deep core the idea of inclusion. Its core belief rested in the need for the inclusion of poor and marginalized populations in all levels of education. Along these lines, the Ministry of Education created inclusive policies for illiterate adults, indigenous populations, *quilombolas*,[15] prison inmates, and significantly expanded access to higher education for low-income students. It also strengthened and expanded policies to help poor students remain in school, like the national school feeding program and the free-of-charge textbook program.

The MoE coalition combined its inclusion-based deep core with assessment and accountability policy tools. Student performance is nationally assessed at all levels,[16] as well as school performance.[17] Due to the decentralized nature of the education system in Brazil, the ministry decided not to interfere in pedagogical aspects at the local level, but rather to assess the quality of each school and establish quality targets for them.

The second advocacy coalition, which was critical of the MoE coalition but not dramatically opposed to it, is the one formed by civil society organizations and teachers' unions. This coalition is also pro-inclusion and values some of the policies adopted by the Ministry of Education, especially the rise and equalization of education funding brought by Fundeb—Fund for the Maintenance and Development of Basic

Education and the Valorization of Education Professionals. However, the coalition believes that although most of the adopted policies were positive, they were not sufficient to meet the existing needs. It questions the emphasis on standardized exams as the only measure of student performance, as well as on IDEB as the only measure of school performance. This coalition rather points to the importance of investing in teacher training and asks for higher shares of public spending for education (interviewee C14).

Third, there is a coalition of scholars and political opponents to the Workers' Party (PT) that argues that more assessments are needed, as well as more policy evaluations. This coalition also advocates for teacher merit-pay and the establishment of partnerships between public and private schools, whereby private school chains provide public schools with their teaching methods and textbooks (interviewee C11). Since Dilma Rousseff's impeachment in April 2016, this third coalition has conquered space and is likely to replace the education coalition that was at the Ministry of Education during the PT years. The new federal government, led by President Michel Temer, has initiated a reform process in secondary education and has proposed a 20-year freeze on government spending, proposals that are very much aligned with this coalition's deep core.

On *Bolsa Familia*, the later MoE coalition considered that the program was important in providing the means for poor children to have access to school. In contrast, the other two coalitions argue that the program has clear limits in terms of its contribution to education. For them, Brazil's educational problem is not one of demand, but rather of the quality of supply. Members of these coalitions argue that families do not send children to school because the taught contents are not relevant, because teachers are often absent, and because families cannot envision the importance of schooling for their children's lives (interviewees C11 and C14).

Outside of education, coalitions have also been formed around social protection policies. The dominating coalition during most of *Bolsa Familia's* years, which was ahead of the program at the Ministry of Social Development (MDS), has in its deep core the principles of citizenship and social rights. Its core belief is that cash transfers help the poor exercise their citizenship and rights to education and health services. Consequently, program conditionalities were not meant to be incentives for behavior and should not result in the "punishment" of noncompliant families. Rather, in cases of noncompliance, conditionalities should work as triggers for additional government action to support vulnerable families. Local governments were expected to follow-up on the reasons for noncompliance and help families get back on track (interviewees C18 and C19). The later MDS coalition advocated for the unification of cash transfers in Brazil, for the importance of targeting, conditionalities, and the Single Registry.

Second, there is the Minimum Income coalition. Led by Senator Eduardo Suplicy and supported by scholars such as Lena Lavinas, this coalition defends the implementation of the 2004 Minimum Income law, which should result in a universal and unconditional cash transfer program. This coalition, however, is not combative of *Bolsa Família*. Senator Suplicy also belongs to the Workers' Party and publicly acknowledges the importance of the program and what it has done to poverty reduction in Brazil. Besides, a compromise has been reached in which *Bolsa Família* is to be the first step toward the achievement of a universal minimum income policy (interviewee C13).

Third, a coalition has been formed around the past experience of *Bolsa Escola*. Its deep core is based on the fundamental importance of education for poverty reduction and development. Its core belief is that lack of income leads poor families to send their children to work rather than to school. Consequently, these families should receive a "salary" that compensates them for keeping children in school. Simultaneously, the government ought to make even higher investments in the quality of schools attended by *Bolsa* recipients (interviewee C15).

Interestingly, the above three coalitions share the premise that Brazilian society has been historically so unequal that it has a "social debt" to its poor (Lindert et al. 2007). Consequently, according to them the government has the duty of designing social protection policies that will redistribute a part of the country's wealth while making sure that families can invest in children's education to improve the country's future prospects.

Besides the above-mentioned coalitions, whose representatives were interviewed as part of this study, Cotta (2009) describes three other "visions about social protection"[18] (p. 63) and their standpoint *vis-à-vis* conditional cash transfers. First, there is the food security vision, which is defended by civil society organizations, those who were ahead of the Zero Hunger program, and those at the Department of Food and Nutritional Security at MDS. According to this vision, food and nutritional security are the first and major issues to be tackled by social protection policies in

Brazil. It was shared by the coalition that dominated the first year of the Lula administration and was later replaced by the *Bolsa Família* coalition. Although those in the "food security coalition" used to argue that cash transfers had limitations and did not allow people's empowerment, they increasingly accepted *Bolsa Família* as a part of Zero Hunger, which was turned into a broader, long-term strategy.

Furthermore, Cotta (2009) describes the vision of social protection that focuses on social assistance rights. Social workers, some scholars, and some government officials are the ones who share this vision, arguing that social assistance services shall be at the core of a comprehensive policy of social protection. The coalition that portrays this vision was very critical of CCT programs during the Cardoso administration (1995–2002), relating CCTs to the structural adjustment reforms of the 1990 s. However, with the rise of a Left-leaning government and the creation of *Bolsa Família* by PT, the "social assistance coalition" reconsidered its position toward CCTs. It is still reluctant to accept them as a comprehensive public policy, but concede to their importance as poverty-reduction programs. This coalition used to permeate the Department of Social Assistance at MDS, as well as many Departments of Social Assistance in municipal governments. Consequently, its acquiescence is very important to assure that the program is adequately managed at the local level.

Third, Cotta (2009) finds the "social spending vision," according to which *Bolsa Família* is simply seen as a type of social spending. Those who follow this vision are mostly concerned about the equilibrium of national accounts. In that framework, conditional cash transfers stand out as noncontributory direct transfers, as they are not based on individual contributions (like social security) and do not depend on intermediary institutions for payments to be delivered. This vision is mostly espoused by some scholars, researchers, and government officials outside the field of social development/protection. Since their goal is not primarily to dominate policymaking in social protection, it can be argued that this vision has not translated into a mobilized advocacy coalition.

Lastly, is the coalition that completely discredits *Bolsa Família* and often calls the program *BolsaEsmola* (charity stipend). This coalition's deep core is based on the idea of meritocracy. Its core belief is that the poor should work harder in order to increase their income and that the country's economy should grow in order to make jobs available to everyone. The coalition opposes income redistribution and argues that *Bolsa Família* solely serves political purposes and makes the poor welfare-dependent. Again, this is a coalition that has recently gained more political space and power, especially since the presidential impeachment process and the ousting of the Workers' Party from the federal government. An example of its increased influence has been the recent decision of the Ministry of Social and Agrarian Development (MDSA, formerly MDS), to scrutinize the information about all *Bolsa Família* beneficiaries, in order to identify inconsistencies and exclude beneficiaries from the program. This process has led to the exclusion of 469,000 beneficiary families (MDSA 2016b).

In analyzing how *Bolsa Família* may have altered the power balance between the advocacy coalitions in dispute, it was found that the program's scale, impact, and resulting political strength ended up giving significant force to the coalitions "in office" during the PT years—especially those coalitions that were at the MoE and *Bolsa Família*'s Department of Citizen's Income at MDS. However, with recent changes in the Brazilian federal government, new coalitions have acceded to power, which may further erode the weak link between *Bolsa Família* and policies for improved education quality.

6.7   A Political Phenomenon

As reported above, *Bolsa Família* is at the center of the dispute among several advocacy coalitions in the field of social development/protection. However, except for the coalition that completely despises the program, much of that dispute was not about whether *Bolsa Família* should continue or not. The debate was rather about the program's place in the social protection policy, the purpose it should serve, whether it should be conditional or not, targeted or universal, and whether and how it should create exit strategies for beneficiary families.[19]

Consequently, the "victory" of *Bolsa Família*'s coalition over most others for over 10 years took place through the accommodation of interests rather than through confrontation. Again, except for the extreme media critics, all other coalitions accepted that the program was there to stay and that they had to adjust their discourse. This was only possible because, as also verified in Colombia, the CCT model is adjustable to various belief systems.

At the time of the interviews, which took place before the abrupt end of the Rousseff administration, no single interviewee raised doubts about *Bolsa Família*'s survival. In fact, interviewee C15 affirmed: "no politician would dare to propose the termination of Bolsa Família." Thus, the program's political sustainability was out of the question. This issue will be further explored by making use of the conceptual tools provided by the punctuated-equilibrium theory and the civic capacity framework.

6.7.1   Punctuated-Equilibrium

Different from the other two programs in this study, which were part of a broader policy monopoly, one could say that *Bolsa Família* is the policy monopoly itself. The program has consolidated a monopoly on political understandings of how the government of Brazil shall combat poverty in the country. It was not only backed by a strong policy venue—the Ministry of Social Development, it was strongly backed by two Presidents—Lula and Dilma Rousseff—and possibly a third now—Michel Temer.

Bolsa Família can strongly count on the main elements identified by PET for the maintenance of a policy monopoly over time: attention and a positive policy image. Following the analysis of the Dow Jones Factiva database, a total of 8252 articles were published on *Bolsa Família* between 2007 and 2009, in all languages. Of those, 7167 were published by the Brazilian press. Such a high level of media attention is confirmed by Lindert (2007), who used the World Bank Media Database on Conditional Cash Transfers. Lindert searched six major Brazilian newspapers from 2001 to 2006 and found over 6,500 articles on at least one of Brazil's conditional cash transfer programs.[20] In 2006, there was an average of one article in each newspaper every day (Lindert 2007).

Baumgartner and Jones (2005) argue that attention is highly important, but a positive tone is fundamental to assure a positive policy image and maintain a policy monopoly. In this regard, *Bolsa Família* was very fortunate during most of its years of existence. In the 2007–2009 appraisal, of over 8000 newspaper articles, only 30 included the word controversial/*controverso/controvertido* and 198 included the word critics/*critico*. Lindert (2007) also found that 44% of all articles had a positive tone and only 6% were fully negative.

Although there is a high chance that this dominant positive attention may have recently weakened, especially with the strengthening of conservative political forces in the country, the program maintains its policy monopoly and has been able to survive, despite the major changes in government that occurred after Rousseff's oust in April 2016.

6.7.2   Civic Capacity

Although it was not possible to carry out school interviews, some interviewees said they believed there was high teacher support to *Bolsa Familia* (interviewee C8). Additionally, the above-reported high levels of media attention and the dominating positive tone were representative of the population's overall support to *Bolsa Familia*. In 2007, Ipsos carried out an opinion poll of the Lula administration. When asked about what Lula had done well in office, 43% of respondents indicated "*Bolsa Familia*" as their first answer (cited in Lindert 2007).

Positive perceptions about *Bolsa Familia* have to some extent translated into political support to the Workers' Party and local governments. In 2006, Ipsosalso did a quantitative analysis of the characteristics of respondents who favored the Lula government. It found that being a beneficiary of social programs was highly correlated with favoring the government (cited in Lindert 2007). Also, De Janvry et al. (2008, cited in Lindert 2007) analyzed the 2004 municipal election results in the Northeast of Brazil. In municipalities where the incumbent mayor was re-elected for a second term, researchers found that *Bolsa Familia* had higher coverage rates and better targeting accuracy.

Lindert (2007) argues that the high levels of political support to *Bolsa Familia* are a result of the combination between three factors: implementation, impacts, and politics. The program's implementation has been fairly efficient, discrediting accusations of political manipulation. Besides, research evidence has shown that *Bolsa Familia* has had considerable positive impacts. For instance, Barros et al. (2007) found that the program was responsible for 41% of the reduction in income inequality between 2005 and 2006. It was also responsible for 25% of the reduction in extreme poverty between 2001 and 2005.

Despite *Bolsa Familia's* major role in poverty reduction and inequality reduction in the country, growing conservative forces have accused the government of creating welfare dependence and of "buying" votes through welfare programs. Until recently, these forces had been isolated and did not represent a threat to the program's survival. However, as these forces gain space in the Parliament, in the Judiciary, and in the new Temer government, there is no absolute guarantee that civic capacity around the program will remain strong.

6.8   POLICY BORROWING: NO NEED TO BORROW

CCTs have existed for the longest time in Brazil and they did not emerge out of processes of policy borrowing from abroad. However, that does not mean *Bolsa Familia* might not have been influenced by foreign models. In fact, the very decision to create *Bolsa Familia* by unifying previously existing CCTs was to some extent influenced by advice from *Oportunidades'* creator Santiago Levy (interviewee C6). Also, *Bolsa Familia* officials have been part of the international network of CCT specialists, who meet regularly in countless meetings for experience sharing.

Even so, there is no explicit evidence of policy borrowing from a particular country. MDS officials consider that Brazil has numerous peculiarities and has been attempting to cope with them on its own. Only recently has the *Bolsa Familia* team made a concession to import some aspects of Chile's CCT, particularly the processes of family follow-up and case management (interviewee C17).

Such a lack of efforts to borrow from elsewhere may be explained by *Bolsa Familia's* long-lived legitimacy in Brazil, as detailed above. Just as the borrowing and lending literature predicts that policymakers borrow policy models from elsewhere in order to obtain legitimacy to their own proposals at home, governments that enjoy significant support for their policies may be in the comfortable position of not having to borrow. That seemed to have been the case in *Bolsa Familia*.

The absence of policy borrowing does not mean that Brazil has not received foreign support, particularly from donors. The World Bank has been the program's most important external partner. As explained earlier, the bank played an important role in *Bolsa Familia's* creation by convincing the Brazilian government to base its poverty-reduction strategy on targeted conditional cash transfers rather than on unconditional food support (interviewees C2 and C6).

Following the unification of programs and the "birth" of *Bolsa Familia*, the World Bank negotiated and approved a new loan to support the program. The "*Bolsa Familia* First Adaptable Program Loan" involved a total budget of US$520 million and was approved in June 2004 (World Bank 2004). Most loan funds—US$500 million—were to be directly used for family cash transfers. Interestingly, the loan had a performance-based mechanism in which funds were disbursed according to the pace of family payments. The creation of such a mechanism was intended to guarantee that Brazil's treasury would make resources available to the program (interviewee C2).

The remaining part of the loan was aimed at technical assistance activities, such as strengthening the system to identify the target population; developing a monitoring and evaluation system; institutional strengthening; and project management (World Bank 2004). One of the bank's important technical contributions to *Bolsa Familia* has been the publication of the most comprehensive working papers written in English about the program. For instance, the paper entitled "The nuts and bolts of Brazil's *Bolsa Familia* Program," by Lindert et al. (2007), explains the program operations in great detail.

The Inter-American Development Bank (IDB) also provided the program with financial support in its early stages (Hall 2008). In 2009, the IDB approved a new *Bolsa Familia*-related project, this time aimed at knowledge building and sharing in the broader field of social protection. The project, with a budget of only US$1 million, is described as:

> The Technical cooperation [TC] will support the definition of the country's mid and long-term strategy in social protection. The TC will finance studies, seminars and workshops that will feed into a Knowledge Agenda for (i) the evaluation of the social safety net in Brazil, (ii) the definition of strategies for including families in vulnerability in urban areas and metropolitan regions; and (iii) identification and analysis of best practices for the economic inclusion of beneficiaries in productive and income-generating activities. (IDB 2010)

The UK's Department for International Development (DFID) has been another constant partner of *Bolsa Familia*. DFID has offered direct technical assistance and has hired consultants to work in the program. Recently, it has provided technical and financial support for sharing of social protection experiences between MDS and the African countries (see section below).

Interestingly, donors have changed their approach toward Brazil and *Bolsa Familia* in recent years. According to interviewee C17, in the beginning of the Lula administration donors used to approach MDS to offer technical assistance and financial support. In some cases, there were strings attached to their offers and they presented specific demands on how projects should be developed. Recently, however, the ministry has been given greater voice in cooperation initiatives. Besides, donors such as DFID and the World Bank have increasingly asked MDS to share its experience with other countries. As concluded by interviewee C17, this new situation reflects how *Bolsa Familia* in particular and the government of Brazil as a whole have gained international respect in recent years.

6.9   Policy Lending: High Demand

Since the idea of a conditional cash transfer program has existed in Brazil since the 1990s, there have been countless opportunities of policy lending involving Brazilian CCT idealizers and policymakers. In fact, proponents of the different variations of cash transfer schemes have made use of policy lending to earn legitimacy for their ideas. For instance, *Bolsa Escola* creators claim a direct influence over the establishment of similar CCTs in Latin America, such as those in Mexico, Ecuador, and in the city of Buenos Aires (Aguiar and Araújo 2002). In the case of Mexico's *Progresa/Oportunidades*, Brazilian interviewees reported that Mexican officials visited Brazil to get to know the *Bolsa Escola* experience (interviewees C4 and C15).[21] Additionally, Cristovam and his supporters created the NGO *Missão Criança* (Mission Child), aimed at the promotion of the *Bolsa Escola* model. The NGO has supported the creation of pilot *Bolsa Escola* programs in other countries, such as Mozambique, Guatemala, Sao Tome and Principe, and Tanzania (Missão Criança 2010).

Advocates of a universal minimum income have also made international efforts to lend the idea to other countries. Senator Suplicy, for instance, has promoted his proposal for a basic/minimum income in countries such as Cuba, Ireland, Argentina, Uruguay, Iraq, Bangladesh, and Mozambique (interviewee C13). As part of these efforts, the 2010 international meeting of the Basic Income Earth Network (BIEN) was held in Brazil.

Since the creation of *Bolsa Familia* the government of Brazil has received various cooperation requests from other developing countries. As the program has been well documented in the international CCT literature, governments around the world have received information about it. Many have developed an interest in getting to know it in greater detail and in possibly importing its model.

Bolsa Familia's policy lending initiatives were for various years a result of Lula's foreign policy agenda. During his visits to other developing countries, as well as during visits by other presidents and prime ministers, Lula often offered technical cooperation in the field of social development and poverty reduction. As a result, various bilateral Protocols of Intention were signed. Then, if the cooperating country demonstrated interest, specific projects were designed by the Brazilian Cooperation Agency (ABC) and by the Ministry of Social Development, in which Brazilian funds were made available to transfer the *Bolsa Familia* experience.

Different from *Bolsa Escola's* proponents and those who advocate for a basic income for all citizens, *Bolsa Familia's* managers and supporters have not had to actively seek to promote the program abroad. The first reason is that *Bolsa Familia* was for many years politically strong in Brazil, as discussed above. Thus, the program did not need the seal of approval that comes with policy lending (Steiner-Khamsi 2004). Second, foreign demand for *Bolsa Familia* was so high that MDS mostly worked in a responsive manner. Third, as the ministry counts on limited human resources to manage the program—about 200 people, as opposed to almost 1,000 working for Mexico's *Oportunidades*, for instance, there was not much available personnel to work on lending the program model to other countries (interviewee C17). Consequently, MDS cannot devote much resources and energy to replicating *Bolsa Familia* elsewhere.

Donors have played an important role in encouraging the international diffusion of the *Bolsa Familia* model. The World Bank, for instance, has worked as a "bridge" institution, linking Brazil to other countries that are interested in establishing a CCT or that already have one. That was the case of India and Peru. Besides providing resources to fund exchanges between countries, the bank also offers a loan to help fund the creation of a CCT in the recipient country (interviewee C1). The bank has also encouraged Brazil's own South–South Cooperation efforts. In March 2010, the bank organized a conference in Colombia in order to promote the sharing of South–South Cooperation practices. MDS was invited to participate and to specifically present its South–South Cooperation experiences involving *Bolsa Familia*.

The UK's Department for International Development (DFID) has also been very active in supporting the cooperation between Brazil and other developing countries in the field of social protection. Specifically, DFID financed the "Africa-Brazil Cooperation Program on Social Development." DFID's program facilitated cooperation efforts between Brazil and selected African countries, constituting a so-called triangulation initiative in South–South Cooperation. Although the program's mission was broadly defined in terms of social development, there have been initiatives specifically focused on *Bolsa Familia*. According to the Africa–Brazil website, housed by the International Policy Center for Inclusive Growth (IPC-IG) :

> In 2006, representatives of Ghana, Guinea Bissau, Mozambique, Nigeria, South Africa and Zambia undertook a study tour to Brazil on conditional cash transfer programs. In 2007, Brazil provided the government of Ghana with technical cooperation in the design of a pilot social grants program entitled Livelihood Empowerment Against Poverty. (IPC-IG 2010)

Despite such a high demand from other countries and interest from donors, *Bolsa Familia* has not obtained as much international exposure as Mexico's *Progresa/Oportunidades*, especially in the academic literature (interviewee C3). Major CCT funders such as the World Bank and the Inter-American Development Bank have also featured the Mexican CCT many more times than Brazil's *Bolsa* programs (*Bolsa Escola and Bolsa Família*). Figure 6.2 presents the number of entries found on the banks' websites for Brazil's and Mexico's CCTs up to 2010.

When asked about why *Progresa/Oportunidades* is better known internationally than *Bolsa Família*, interviewees indicated the following reasons:

1. "*Bolsa Familia* is so Brazilian." It works in a decentralized way and only uses the self-declared family income as its targeting criterion (interviewee C1).
2. Most evaluations of *Bolsa Familia* have been done on a small scale and quietly, whereas *Oportunidades/Progressa* set up an evaluation unit since its beginning and has made its evaluations internationally available (interviewee C3 and C18).
3. Most Mexican policymakers have studied in US universities. Upon their return they are very serious about applying what they learned in terms of methods and new ideas. Consequently, Mexico ends up becoming a "policy laboratory," which, due to its link with the US, gets significant international visibility (interviewee C7).
4. *Progresa/Oportunidades* has been more dependent on international funding than *Bolsa Familia* (interviewee C7).
5. *Progressa/Oportunidades* has strictly conformed to the CCT model that international experts have advocated for: it is completely focused on building human capital, which is reflected on the program design, documents, and discourse (interviewee C18).

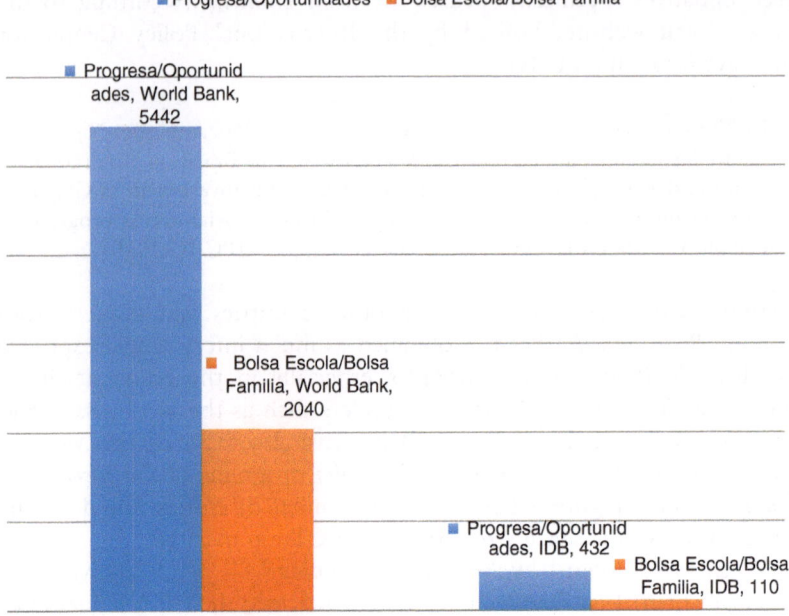

Fig. 6.2 *Progresa/Oportunidades* and *Bolsa Escola/Bolsa Família* on the Banks' websites

Furthermore, interviewee C7 argued that *Progresa–Oportunidades* has faced greater political challenges at home than *Bolsa Família*. Although Mexico is also a federation, its CCT has been designed and implemented in a centralized way. In order to obtain legitimacy, especially in the relationship with different states, the program has needed the "international seal of approval." On the other hand, the decentralized implementation of *Bolsa Família* has allowed the sharing of "political dividends" between the federal, state, and municipal governments. Consequently, the program is supported by a multipartisan network and is less in need of external legitimation.

Since the creation of *Bolsa Família*, all governmental policy lending initiatives on CCTs have been carried out by the Ministry of Social Development. Although the Ministry of Education developed a system for conditionality monitoring of considerable quality, it has not participated in international CCT cooperation initiatives. On the other hand, the MoE has been the protagonist of South–South Cooperation efforts in various other fields, such as adult literacy, teacher training, assessment and accountability, and financing of education.

NOTES

1. Which corresponds to 28 billion Brazilian Reais, considering an exchange rate of 1:4.
2. Recently renamed Ministério do Desenvolvimento Social e Agrário (MDSA—Ministry of Social and Agrarian Development).
3. In Brazil the President may create new legal instruments that have the status of law but do not need to be pre-approved by Congress in order to have immediate effectiveness. They are called *Medidas Provisórias* (Provisional Measures). Once a Provisional Measure is signed by the President, Congress is given a deadline to vote it and the Measure takes priority on the legislative agenda.
4. States and municipalities.
5. Considering an average exchange rate for 2016 of US$ 1: R$ 3.30.
6. Extremely poor families, or those with a monthly income per capita of up to 85 reais, are eligible to receiving the basic transfer regardless of the presence of children in the household.
7. Poor families, or those with a monthly income per capita ranging from 85 to 170 reais, are only eligible to the variable transfers. In order to be eligible to the program, there should be children up to 17 years old in the household or a pregnant or nursing woman.
8. The maximum transfer amount that can be perceived by a poor beneficiary family corresponds to less than half a minimum wage. In contrast, initial local CCTs such as the Federal District's Bolsa Escola used to transfer one minimum wage per beneficiary family per month.
9. The Single Registry (*Cadastro Único*) is a national database that houses information on beneficiaries of federal social programs. It is a core tool for the effective functioning of Bolsa Familia, as it provides the pool of eligible families out of which program participants are randomly selected and concentrates all available information on Bolsa Familia beneficiaries.
10. The Single Registry coverage rate corresponds to the ratio between the number of families living in a municipality who are registered in the Single Registry and the total number of families in that municipality who would qualify for registration.
11. This number has been included in the IGD formula in order to boost the amount to be transferred to small municipalities.

12. Since Bolsa Escola and the Campinas program, Brazil's CCTs have maintained the policy of issuing payments to the female head of the household. Research evidence indicates that mothers are better than fathers in spending the money according to the needs of children, although this practice has raised all sorts of debates around whether it increases women's multiple burdens.

13. At the Ministry of Education the system is under the responsibility of the Department of Lifelong Learning, Literacy, Diversity and Inclusion (SECADI).

14. Brazilian public schools may be under the control either of the state government or of the municipal government. Consequently, most municipalities have a mix of state and municipal schools. However, for the purposes of Bolsa Familia, the municipal government is the one responsible for reporting class attendance of all students, regardless of the kind of public school where they are enrolled.

15. Quilombolas are members of traditional communities founded by slaves who escaped farms and settled in remote areas.

16. Student assessments include Provinha Brazil (Brazil's Little Exam), Prova Brazil (Brazil Exam), the National High School Exam (ENEM), and the National Assessment of Student Performance (ENADE).

17. Each public school in Brazil has its performance measured through the Index of Basic Education Development (IDEB). It is a composite index based on students' performance on national assessments and on the school's average repetition rate. IDEB is calculated every two years and leads to the establishment of quality improvement targets for each school.

18. Cotta's concept of visions about social protection is close to Sabatier and Jenkins-Smith's advocacy coalition framework. She argues that the visions about social protection are espoused by communities of thought, which are defined as "groups of people that share a normative and cognitive base and a certain style of thought" (p. 64). The subtle difference between 'visions' and 'advocacy coalitions' is that members of advocacy coalitions strive to dominate policymaking in order to materialize their core beliefs. In the case of visions of social protection, communities of thought are simply clustered around their shared visions.

19. Currently, Bolsa Familia does not have a time limit for family participation in the program. As long as families meet eligibility criteria, comply with conditionalities, and update their information in the Single Registry every two years, they can indefinitely continue receiving program benefits.

20. Lindert (2007) was interested in media coverage on Bolsa Familia, as well as on its predecessors.

21. However, Santiago Levy, the founder of Progresa/Oportunidades in Mexico, does not mention Bolsa Escola as a source of inspiration in Levy (2006).

REFERENCES

Aguiar, M., & Araújo, C. H. (2002). *Bolsa Escola: Education to confront poverty*. Brasilia: UNESCO.

Barros, R. P. D., Carvalho, M. D., Franco, S., & Mendonça, R. (2007). *Determinantes imediatos da queda da desigualdade de renda brasileira* (Texto para discussão n. 1253). Rio de Janeiro: IPEA.

Bastagli, F. (2008). *The design, implementation and impact of conditional cash transfers targeted on the poor: An evaluation of Brazil's Bolsa Família*. Unpublished manuscript. London School of Economics and Political Science, London.

Baumgartner, F., Jones, B. (2005). The politics of attention: How government prioritizes problems. Chicago: University of Chicago Press.

Brazil. (1996). *National Educational Bases and Guidelines Law*. Retrieved February 24, 2010, from http://www.planalto.gov.br/ccivil_03/Leis/L9394.htm.

Britto, T. F. (2004). *Conditional cash transfers: Why have they become so prominent in recent poverty reduction strategies in Latin America?* The Hague: Institute of Social Studies.

Campello, T., Falcão, T., & Costa, P. (2014). *O Brasil sem Miséria*. Brasília: Ministério do Desenvolvimento Social e Combate à Fome.

Cotta, T. C. S. (2009). *Visões de proteção social e transferências de renda condicionadas no Brasil e no México* (Views on social protection and conditional cash transfer programs in Brazil and México). Unpublished doctoral dissertation, University of Brasília.

De la Briere, B., Hobbs, J., Linder, A., & Lindert, K. (2007). *The impacts of the Bolsa Família Program: A meta-review of conditional cash transfers in Brazil*. Unpublished manuscript.

Draibe, S. (2003). A política social no período FHC e o sistema de proteção social. *Tempo social, 15*(2), 63–101.

De Janvry, A., Finan, F., Sadoulet, E. (2008). *Local electoral accountability and decentralized performance*. Unpublished manuscript.

Escola Nacional de Administração Pública. (2010). *Concurso inovação na gestão pública federal: Resumo das iniciativas ordenadas pelo número de inscrição* (Award Innovation in Federal Public Management: Summary of initiatives by registration number). Retrieved March 01, 2010, from http://inovacao.enap.gov.br/images/Documentos/resumos.pdf.

Glewwe, P., & Kassouf, A. (2008). *The impact of the Bolsa Escola/Bolsa Família conditional cash transfer program on enrollment, drop out rates and grade promotion in Brazil*. Unpublished manuscript.

Hall, A. (2008). Brazil's Bolsa Familia: A double-edged sword? *Development and change, 39*(5), 799–822.

Hellman, A. G. (2015). *How does Bolsa Familia work? Best practices in the implementation of conditional cash transfers in Latin America and the Caribbean* (Technical

Note No.IDB-TN-856). Washington, DC: Inter-American Development Bank.

IDB. (2010). *BR-T1080: Knowledge agenda—Social protection.* Retrieved March 8, 2010, from http://www.iadb.org/projects/project.cfm?id=BR-T1080& lang=en.

IPC-IG. (2010). *Africa-Brazil Cooperation Programme on Social Development.* Retrieved March 5, 2010, from http://www.ipc-undp.org/ipc/africa-brazil.jsp.

Levy, S. (2006). *Progress against poverty: Sustaining Mexico's Progresa-Oportunidades program.* Washington, DC: Brookings Institution Press.

Lindert, K. (2007). Brazil's Bolsa Familia Program: Two and a half presentations on implementation, impacts, and perceptions. Presentation at Georgetown University, 26 September 2007.

Lindert, K., Linder, A., Hobbs, J., & de la Briere, B. (2007). The nuts and bolts of Brazil's Bolsa Família program: Implementing conditional cash transfers in a descentralized context. *World Bank Social Protection Discussion Paper, 709.* Washington, DC: World Bank.

MDS. (2008). Programa Bolsa Familia. Retrieved November 2, 2008, from http://www.mds.gov.br/bolsafamilia/.

MDS. (2010a). *Índice de Gestão Descentralizada* (Index of Decentralized Management). Retrieved March 2, 2010, from http://www.mds.gov.br/ bolsafamilia/estados_e_municipios/estados_e_municipios/indice-de-gestao-descentralizada-igd.

MDS. (2010b). *Municípios receberão R$ 22.5 milhões para investir na gestão do Bolsa Família* (Municipalities will receive 22.5 million reais to invest in the management of Bolsa Família). Retrieved March 2010, from http://www. mds.gov.br/bolsafamilia/noticias/municipios-receberao-r-22-5-milhoes-para-investir-na-gestao-do-bolsa-familia.

MDS. (2010c). *Descumprimento de condicionalidades* (Failure to comply with conditionalities). Retrieved March 3, 2010, from http://www.mds.gov.br/ bolsafamilia/condicionalidades/advertencias-e-sancoes.

MDSA. (2016a). *Bolsa Família: acompanhamento da frequência escolar alcança 91.8% dos beneficiários.* Retrieved November 19, 2016, from http://mds.gov. br/area-de-imprensa/noticias/2016/novembro/bolsa-familia-acompanha-mento-da-frequencia-escolar-alcanca-91-8-dos-beneficiarios.

MDSA. (2016b). *Pente-fino no Bolsa Família encontra irregularidades em 1,1mil-hão de benefícios.* Retrieved November 19, 2016, from http://mds.gov.br/ area-de-imprensa/noticias/2016/novembro/pente-fino-no-bolsa-familia-encontra-irregularidades-em-1-1-milhao-de-beneficios.

Missão Criança. (2010). *Atuação internacional* (International action). Retrieved on March 5, 2010, from http://www.missaocrianca.org.br/saibamais.html.

Paiva, L. H., Soares, F. V., Cireno, F., Viana, I. A. V., & Duran, A. C. (2016). The effects of conditionality monitoring (Working Paper No. 144). Brasília: International Policy Center for Inclusive Growth.

Steiner-Khamsi, G. (2004). *The politics of educational borrowing and lending.* New York: Teachers College Press.

The Economist. (2007, April 12). Rich man, poor man. Special report: Brazil. *The Economist.*

World Bank. (2004). *Project Information Document. Bolsa Familia First Adaptable Program Loan.* Retrieved March 8, 2010, from http://www-wds.worldbank.org/external/default/WDSContentServer/WDSP/IB/2004/05/11/000104615_20040513125107/Rendered/PDF/BF0PID0100MAY02004.pdf.

World Bank. (2010). *Key development data and statistics.* Retrieved February 19, 2010, from http://web.worldbank.org/WBSITE/EXTERNAL/DATASTATISTICS/0,,contentMDK:20535285~menuPK:1192694~pagePK:64133150~piPK:64133175~theSitePK:239419,00.html.

Yonemura, A., (2005). *The changing social agenda in Brazil: An analysis of the policymaking process in the case of Bolsa Escola.* Unpublished doctoral dissertation, Teachers College, Columbia University.

PART III

What Have We Learned?

CHAPTER 7

Case Comparison: CCTs' Divorce from Education Policy and Long Program Lives

Data collection and analysis across three very different conditional cash transfers (CCTs) have allowed this study to, on the one hand, go into the details of their life cycle. Getting to know each program as they emerged, were implemented, and even eventually ended gives the perspective to help in the understanding of the linkages between these poverty reduction programs and education policy. On the other hand, analyzing them comparatively can help one see beyond the peculiarities and idiosyncrasies of each CCT experience and rather identify some common trends. This chapter attempts to add this comparative perspective to previous case-based chapters, so as to explore patterns that are not obvious consequences of the global diffusion process.

7.1   Comparatively Speaking

7.1.1   Does Scale Matter?

The first interesting variable that stood out in the comparison of those three CCT programs was their scale of operation. The figures presented in Table 7.1 give an idea of each program's size and outreach.

One of the interesting conclusions that come out from Table 7.1 is that the number of beneficiaries is not necessarily proportional to the program's budget. Opportunity NYC benefitted a relatively small number of participants but involved a budget of over 50 million dollars during its first two years. Besides its significantly greater amount of transfers,

© The Author(s) 2017
M. Morais de Sá e Silva, *Poverty Reduction, Education, and the Global Diffusion of Conditional Cash Transfers*, DOI 10.1007/978-3-319-53094-9_7

Table 7.1   Scale of operation

	Opportunity NYC	*Subsidios*	*Bolsa Familia*
Year of creation	2007	2004	2003 *Bolsa Escola*: 1995 Guarantee of Minimum Family Income: 1995
Initial number of beneficiaries	2400 families + 8000 students	9749	3.8 million (Lindert et al. 2007)
Current number of beneficiaries	Same	80,000 (expansion to 100,000)	12.4 million families
Budget (PPP[a], million)	53.4 for the first two years	37.07	Around 8220
Maximum payment amount per year (PPP)	650 elementary school 750 middle school 4100–4500 high school	320	1644
Media coverage between 2007 and 2009 (all countries, all languages)	209	4	8252

[a]PPP: Purchasing power parity. Values were calculated using World Bank PPP rates for 2008

the program is also more expensive because of administrative costs. According to Bosman (2010), by the end of the second year of program implementation "$14 million had been paid out to 2400 families. An additional $10.2 million is for operating costs, and $9.6 million for research and evaluation." Although interviewee A7 noted that the program did not get the economies of scale that would appear in a larger CCT, such a high administrative bill should be in the minds of policymakers who may consider the adoption of the Opportunity NYC model.

Also, if *Bolsa Familia* and *Subsidios* are compared, there seems to be a direct relationship between scale and media coverage. Opportunity NYC, however, seems to be an outlier in that regard, as such a small program was featured in over 200 articles even though it benefitted only 2400 families (Family Rewards) plus 8000 students (Spark). Being tested in New York City certainly seems to be a natural reason for increased media exposure, but there could be other factors such as marketing efforts by City Hall and the sponsoring foundations, as well as significant buy-in from international organizations.

Additionally, it looks like scale matters for the emergence of advocacy coalitions specifically disputing the program (rather than disputing the education or social policy as a whole). Small programs such as Opportunity NYC and *Subsidios*, which do not place significant interests at stake, tend to fit into pre-existing advocacy coalitions concerned about bigger policy issues. On the other hand, large-scale programs such as *Bolsa Familia*, which involve great political dividends, lead to the formation of disputing coalitions around their own issues. A large-scale CCT is so important in a country's political scenario that it mobilizes opinions and belief systems that are clustered around different groups. Actually, in the case of *Bolsa Familia* these advocacy coalitions are not formed around beliefs concerning education, but rather around issues pertaining to the program's identity as a poverty reduction strategy. This observation seems to go well with more recent debates on advocacy coalitions and those who argue that coalitions are formed around the policy solution rather than around a belief system (Zittoun 2014).

7.1.2   The Role of International Organizations

Internationally, education specialists have not been involved in studies and evaluations of CCTs or in the management of related projects of international organizations. Among the interviewed staff members of these organizations, the ones who operate education projects indicated that they had not worked with CCT programs and did not have much to say about it. On the other hand, those who had worked closely with CCTs declared that they did not know much about education.

This finding contradicts the fact that most evaluations assess the performance of CCTs in terms of how much they have contributed to raising education indicators. For instance, Evans (2009) reviewed major recent evaluations of *Bolsa Escola/Bolsa Familia*. Of the eight studies he reviewed, five evaluate the program in terms of its contribution to the education of beneficiary children.[1]

This actual divorce between CCTs and education goes against what one would expect from the dominating international discourse surrounding CCTs, which proposes them as innovative poverty-reduction models that involve mechanisms to build human capital by improving beneficiaries' education and health.

Also, rather than conforming to that human-capital CCT model, the three studied CCTs have various peculiarities when it comes to their design, mode of implementation, and their own policy discourse. Comparing the interviews with program managers with those with representatives of international organizations (as well as with the international literature on the topic), it was surprising to find that the program managers did not completely reproduce the international discourse on CCTs. As a matter of fact, the idea of building human capital was not mentioned by the program managers of any of the three cases.

In Brazil, the dominating discourse is that of citizenship, with conditionalities seen as "co-responsibilities" and even as rights. In Bogota, there is a predominant idea of promoting student well-being by providing children and adolescents with additional income to cope with school expenses and satisfy other daily needs. And Opportunity NYC works around the idea of "rewards" and "incentives" for increased student effort and parental participation. As an example of the disconnect between the international focus on human capital and the individual national discourses, here is an excerpt of how the Ministry of Social Development officially defines *Bolsa Familia*:

> The Bolsa Familia Program is based on the articulation among three dimensions that are essential to overcome poverty and hunger: immediate poverty relief through the direct transfer of income to families; the reinforcement of basic social rights in the fields of Health and Education, by means of the compliance with conditionalities, which help families break the intergenerational cycle of poverty; and the coordination with complementary programs, which are aimed at families' development, so that Bolsa Familia's beneficiaries will be able to overcome their situation of vulnerability and poverty. (MDS 2008)

Thus, although the borrowing and lending literature indicates that policy borrowing occurs mostly at the level of "policy talk" (Steiner-Khamsi 2004), in this case even "policy talk" has been just partially borrowed. The reproduction of the CCT jargon only takes place when it is convenient, such as in international meetings, publications, and loan documents. Domestically, however, each government has produced its own way of conceptualizing and communicating CCT fundamentals.

Considering that the three cases have either worked with international funding (*Subsidios* and *Bolsa Familia*) or have capitalized on international organizations' seal of approval (Opportunity NYC), the above finding would be unexpected from the point of view of the economics of policy borrowing. However, this research was able to identify that in countries such as Brazil and Colombia, which are not extremely poor, governments have some room to impose their will because it is also in the banks' interest to lend money. Such a "reverse dependence" (banks dependent on borrowing governments) was clear in the Colombian case, where banks' ties with the national government generated constraints for the international promotion of Bogota's CCT program.

7.1.3   CCT Borrowing and Lending

When it comes to whether each CCT has officially borrowed from other countries and whether it has exported its own model, it was found that all the cases partially conformed to what the borrowing and lending literature would predict. However, beyond that, each case also showed peculiar aspects related to their borrowing and lending processes.

In the case of Opportunity NYC, the "borrowing from Mexico" discourse was used as a strategy to obtain legitimacy for the program at home. For the same reason, there has been an urge for policy lending. Initiatives to promote the program abroad were initiated even before its impact was known. The peculiar aspect about Opportunity NYC, however, is that eventually critics attacked the idea of having in NYC a program inspired by a poverty-reduction experience in Mexico, where poverty conditions are supposedly very different. Consequently, program managers needed to reassure the public that the model had been adapted.

In Bogota, *Subsidios* was a clear case of the economics of policy borrowing, where there was reference to CCT model programs in Mexico and in Brazil in order to please donors. However, it was interesting to find that *Subsidios* was a case of "reverse" politics of policy lending. The political dispute between those in the city government and those in the national government has generated constraints to policy lending. International banks have not promoted the program outside of Colombia to prevent upsetting the national government, which has its own CCT program *Familias en Accion*—and which takes annual loans to maintain that program.

Finally, the case of *Bolsa Familia* shows a close connection between findings related to the program's strong political sustainability and its almost lack of policy borrowing. Besides the initial influence by Mexico's experience, *Bolsa Familia* managers have made little efforts to borrow from other CCTs. In theory, until recently, they do not have the political need to. Similarly, there have not been major efforts of policy lending, except for those in response to demands that come directly from other countries or that are intermediated by international organizations.

7.1.4   Similarities Between Pairs of Cases

As a result of the comparison between cases, some features were found to be common only between two of them. For instance, if one looks at Opportunity NYC and *Subsidios*, it is possible to identify that both in New York and in Bogota the CCT program has reinforced the dominating advocacy coalition in education. As they are placed at education institutions—at least formally, they have contributed to adding to the power advocacies "in office". In Brazil, however, that reinforcement did not occur because the program is institutionally and politically very distant from education policymaking. Instead, *Bolsa Familia* involves such high stakes that advocacy coalitions have been formed specifically to dispute the contours of the program itself.

Also, *Subsidios* and Opportunity NYC share the policy decision of not benefitting students in elementary school on the basis of their attendance. In New York that decision also applies to middle school. In Brazil, however, families with children as young as 6-years old are eligible for the cash transfer if their children attend school. Considering that the Brazilian net enrollment rate in primary education reaches 90% as opposed to 81% in secondary education (UIS 2016), the education conditionality does not seem to have a strong role to play for younger kids. This reflects *Bolsa Familia's* focus on reducing income poverty, rather than fulfilling education policy goals.

As for *Subsidios* and *Bolsa Familia*, both in Brazil and in Bogota, critics have questioned the quality of schooling that is being offered to CCT beneficiaries (although that critique has not been turned into organized opposition to the programs). Interestingly, this question has not been raised in the case of Opportunity NYC. One possible reason may be the US drive to raise test scores and the assumption made by some that performance is mostly dependent on individual students' efforts.

Also, in Brazil and in Bogota the programs have a predominant rationale of promoting social rights. In Bogota, the cash transfer's main purpose is the realization of the right to education. And in Brazil, conditionalities are not expected to be incentives for behavior change, as in the case of Opportunity NYC. They are rather seen as policy tools that allow local and federal governments to identify vulnerable families and help them secure their right to education and health services.

Additionally, in both the cases program managers have been strongly concerned about making the selection of beneficiaries a transparent process, making sure that there is little room for accusations of corruption. In Colombia, the first selection of beneficiaries was done as a lottery during a public event to which many stakeholders were invited. In Brazil, beneficiary selection is randomly done with the use of an algorithm. Besides, each municipal government is required to establish a "social control" council formed by representatives of the government and civil society. The council's role is to monitor the implementation of *Bolsa Familia* and make sure that there are no irregularities. Interestingly, corruption and mismanagement have not been a concern in the case of Opportunity NYC.

7.1.5   Individual Peculiarities

Besides each program's peculiar context, history, and *modus operandi*, each of them has other peculiarities that are worth mentioning.

Opportunity NYC has had its experimental nature remarkably emphasized. It also got disproportional media attention, considering that it has been operational for less than 3 years and benefits a relatively small number of families and students. Table 7.2 compares the three programs on the issue of coverage by the media and by the websites of international organizations.

On the other hand, the table also makes it clear that *Subsidios*, despite being just as interesting as the other two CCTs in technical terms, received minimal international coverage. *Subsidios* is also a special case in that it was never a poverty reduction program. It was always meant to be an educational initiative and is viewed as such by policymakers and the public in general. To be sure, *Subsidios* is the only CCT among the three that is institutionally owned by the education "policy subsystem" (True et al. 2007).

In contrast, *Bolsa Familia* is mostly about poverty reduction, despite its origins in the *BolsaEscola* program. In Brazil, compliance with the education conditionalities is not a rigid requirement, but rather a means for beneficiaries to realize a social right. Although the program is serious about duly verifying education conditionalities, failure to comply with

Table 7.2 Case studies coverage by the Media[a] and Multilateral Banks (2007–2009)

	Opportunity NYC	Bolsa Familia	Subsidios
Total number of articles (all languages)	209[b]	8252	4
National articles	168	7167	4
Local articles	97	N/A	4[c]
Indexed under education (all languages)	19	557	2
Controversial/*controvertido/controverso*	20	30	0
Critics/*criticos*	33	198	0
Experiment/experimental	39	0	0
Interesting/*interesante/interessante*	7	160	0
Successful/*exitoso/bem sucedido*	65	199	0
Mexico	109	N/A	N/A
Oportunidades	76	N/A	N/A
World Bank website	96	1210	3
IDB website	1	83	6

[a]According to the Dow Jones Factiva database for the period between 01 January 2007 and 31 December 2009
[b]This number is likely to have significantly increased after the release of the program's impact evaluation on 30 March 2010
[c]All published articles were not only national, but also local (published in Bogota newspapers)

the minimum school attendance does not lead to immediate sanctions. Cash payments are only suspended after a series of notifications to the family and after program efforts have been made to identify the causes of children's absenteeism. That may be, nonetheless, a more comprehensive approach to keeping children in school, since the program is also concerned about the reasons why they miss class.

Finally, it is worth noticing that support or opposition to Bogota's CCT program has been defined along party lines, rather than due to beliefs regarding the principles that animate the program, as was the case in New York. In the case of Brazil, CCTs have been a multipartisan enterprise since the creation of the first local programs in the 1990s. *Bolsa Familia* is *hors concours* and no party or high-profile politician has seriously dared to challenge its existence, even considering the country's current political turmoil.

7.2 CCTs and Policies for Improved Education Quality

As poverty reduction became a part of international and national agendas, education came to be closely related to it, especially following the empirical correlations that can be found between poverty indicators and lack of education. With this idea that education is essential for sustainable poverty reduction, it became increasingly common for education to be viewed not as an end in itself, but as a means for poverty reduction and prevention. Hence, more and better education would be essential for the achievement of developed and less poor societies.

In this framework, as CCTs became internationally prominent and started demonstrating positive impacts in terms of increasing school enrollment and attendance among poor children, higher expectations were created around what they could do for education and, consequently, for the poor. Fiszbein and Schady (2009) state that:

> Although the goals of individual programs vary, most CCTs were created with the expectation that they would help reduce consumption poverty, increase the utilization of health and education services, and result in improvements in final outcomes in schooling, nutrition and health. (p. 160)

Hence, CCT's impact on education is not generally seen as limited to improving access, but also potentially in improving what they call above the "final outcomes in schooling," which means learning, performance, and graduation, among others. Therefore, an important analysis to be made relates to CCT's capacity to influence education policy toward the improvement of education quality. Bearing that in mind, the three cases presented in this book were analyzed through the theories of the policy process, especially those that look at policy change.

However, the three cases studies did not reveal consistent evidence that CCT may have operated as external inducers of change in policies for education quality. First, in none of the cases has the CCT program altered the power balance between education advocacy coalitions in a way that could have caused policy change. Both in Brazil and in Colombia, CCTs rather strengthened the coalitions in office during most of the programs' operation. In New York City, the DoE's lack of ownership over Opportunity NYC—be it in terms of Spark or Family Rewards—made the program neutral *vis-à-vis* education advocacy coalitions.

Second, all the three CCTs were kept separate from policies concerning the improvement of education, from discussions related to learning, or from any other education issues that go beyond indicators of attendance, graduation or, in the case of New York, test scores. Even in the cases where greater integration would be expected (because the Department of Education is responsible for CCT), data showed that the program is either separate from policymaking on education quality at the DoE (the case of *Subsidios*) or is not really implemented by the DoE itself (the case of Opportunity NYC).

Combined with that, in the three cases, education professionals played a limited role—or or no role at all—in the CCT's design or implementation. In New York, Spark was completely managed by economists from Harvard's Education Innovation Laboratory. In Brazil *Bolsa Família* is not managed by the Ministry of Education, is not seen as an education program, and is outside debates on educational issues. Finally, in the *Subsidios* case, program managers do not have an educational background and teachers have not been involved in the program.

Nonetheless, it should be noted that *Subsidios* is the program that, among all the three cases, has achieved the highest level of integration in the field of education. School principals and coordinators have a direct role in the program's operation and are knowledgeable about its purpose and history. As for education scholars and members of teachers' unions, they also know the program in some detail, they have an opinion about it, and are able to link it to other existing policy discussions in education.

Levy (2006) argues that political variables such as some sort of incentive or political enforcement by higher authorities would contribute to increased "symbiosis" between education and CCT programs. However, what the cases under analysis here have shown is that, in practice, these political variables are not currently in place.

7.3   CCT CHANGE AND CONTINUITY

In the framework of the punctuated equilibrium theory it is interesting to notice that the three programs indicate similar patterns. First, the theory is useful to explain the emergence of each CCT despite the peculiarities of each context. Consistently in all the cases, the adoption of the current CCT model occurred within the context of a new administration coming to power and bringing in a new discourse.

In Bogota, the administration that adopted *Subsidios* had a Left-leaning discourse that was very different not only from previous administrations but also from the national government. In New York, Mayor Bloomberg introduced a discourse of innovation and performance-oriented administration that allowed him to try on new strategies. And in Brazil, despite the fact that many accused the Workers' Party administration of simply continuing the policies adopted by its predecessor, the story behind the adoption of *Bolsa Familia* indicates that the program did introduce a new rationale, which cannot be simply thought of as the sum of the preceding programs it unified. Thus, these cases indicate that the adoption of CCTs, as moments of nonincremental policy change, are deeply linked to changes in the surrounding political circumstances (Baumgartner and Jones 1993).

On the other hand, since their first adoption, the three CCTs have maintained a pattern of only incremental change. All of them, since their creation, went through only design-related modifications, such as in the amount of transfers, in the maximum age for beneficiary children, in the mechanisms to enforce compliance with conditionalities, in the selection process of beneficiaries, or in the activities to be rewarded. However, none of those changes considerably changed the nature of the program or the discourse around it. *Bolsa Familia*, which is the case that has existed for the longest time, up to 2016 only went through adjustments meant to make the program more effective in taking the extreme poor out of poverty. And with the beginning of the postimpeachment government in 2016, *Bolsa Familia* has not been affected and for now maintains all the characteristics from the Workers' Party years.

This capacity to survive may be related to the programs' adjustability to different belief systems. In all the cases, CCTs have fit well into the diverging belief systems espoused by various coalitions. In New York City, even potential opponents of Opportunity NYC demonstrated respect for the program due to its experimental nature. CCTs have also been embraced by numerous and even competing political parties, especially in the cases of Colombia and Brazil. In Colombia, even though the city government and the national government belonged to opponent parties at the time of the program creation, each implemented their own CCT program. In Brazil, the first two local CCTs were created by administrations from different parties (PT and PSDB). Then the Cardoso administration created the national *Bolsa Escola*, which was consolidated and expanded in the form of *Bolsa Familia* by the Lula administration. Currently, governments of all Brazilian municipalities, regardless of their political affiliation, have adhered to the program and have collaborated with its local implementation. CCTs' malleability may be part of the explanation of why they are so endurable, as well as why they have rapidly spread to so many countries.

It should be noted, however, that none of the three case-programs are formally guaranteed in the form of a constitutional guarantee. All of them are government programs that do not count on legal assurances that they will be continued by a future administration. *Bolsa Familia* seems to count on strong civic capacity, but the beginning of the post-impeachment administration in the country has made many beneficiaries and program specialists nervous about the program's future. The lack of institutionalization of CCTs has made their funding a big issue for their continuation and expansion, consequently creating dependence upon external funding, be it in the form of international loans or private sponsorships.

NOTE

1. The five studies are: Oliveira (2009), Viana et al. (2009), De Janvry et al. (2008), Bastagli (2008), and Glewwe and Kassouf (2008).

REFERENCES

Bastagli, F. (2008). *The design, implementation and impact of conditional cash transfers targeted on the poor: An evaluation of Brazil's Bolsa Familia.* Unpublished manuscript. London: London School of Economics and Political Science.

Baumgartner, F., & Jones, B. (1993). *Agendas and instability in American politics.* Chicago: University of Chicago Press.

Bosman, J. (2010, March 30). City will stop paying the poor for good behavior. *The New York Times.* Retrieved March 31, 2010, from http://www.nytimes.com/2010/03/31/nyregion/31cash.html?hp.

De Janvry, A., Finan, F., & Sadoulet, E. (2008). *Local electoral accountability and decentralized performance.* Unpublished manuscript.

Fiszbein, A., & Schady, N. (2009). *Conditional cash transfers: Reducing present and future poverty.* Washington, DC: The World Bank Group.

Glewwe, P., & Kassouf, A. (2008). *The impact of the Bolsa Escola/Bolsa Familia conditional cash transfer program on enrollment, drop out rates and grade promotion in Brazil.* Unpublished manuscript.

Levy, S. (2006). *Progress against poverty: Sustaining Mexico's Progresa-Oportunidades program.* Washington, DC: Brookings Institution.

Lindert, K., Linder, A., Hobbs, J., & de la Briere, B. (2007). *The nuts and bolts of Brazil's BolsaFamília program: Implementing conditional cash transfers in a descentralized context.* World Bank Social Protection Discussion Paper, 709. Washington, DC: World Bank.

MDS. (2008). *Programa Bolsa Familia.* Retrieved November 2, 2008, from http://www.mds.gov.br/bolsafamilia/.

Oliveira, A. (2009). *An evaluation of the Bolsa Familia program in Brazil: Expenditures, education and labor outcomes.* Retrieved from http://paa2009. princeton.edu/download.aspx?submissionId=90741.

Steiner-Khamsi, G. (2004). *The politics of educational borrowing and lending.* New York: Teachers College Press.

True, J., Jones, B., & Baumgartner, F. (2007). Punctuated-equilibrium theory: Explaining stability and change in American policymaking. In P. Sabatier (Ed.), *Theories of the policy process.* Boulder: Westview Press.

UIS. (2016). *Brazil Custom Tables.* Retrieved December 3, 2016, from http:// uis.unesco.org/country/br.

Viana, I., Sousa, J., & Oliveira, A. (2009). *Schooling transitions to evaluate the impact of the Bolsa Familia program in Brazil: Breaking the intergenerational cycle of poverty.* Retrieved from http://iussp2009.princeton.edu/download. aspx?submissionId=93015.

Zittoun, P. (2014). *The political process of policymaking: A pragmatic approach to public policy.* New York: Palgrave Macmillan.

CHAPTER 8

Conclusion: What Has the Future Got for This Global Model?

The previous chapter ended on a fairly positive note concerning conditional cash transfers (CCTs) survival and political sturdiness. As a matter of fact, up to 2010, when the first phase of this research was completed, conditional cash transfers looked like an unbeatable policy model. Looking at the various experiences back then, it seemed as if CCTs would be able to survive for as long as there was available funding for them.

The fact that the global CCT model is closer to an idea than to a pre-packaged program, in the sense that it can assume various configurations in terms of beneficiary selection, transfer amount, and set of conditions, makes it resilient to different realities, institutional capacities, and policy goals. No matter what the program design is, if it transfers cash directly to families that have been considered poor on the condition that they perform some human development-related activities, it can be called a CCT.

Also, as discussed in the previous chapter, the permeability of CCTs to a range of different political discourses makes them not only transferrable across various—and even conflicting—political discourses, it also allows them to survive transitions between administrations. That has been the case of various programs in Latin America, which despite significant changes in the political party in office, ended up simply going through slight changes in their design and in the program name. *Familias en Acción* in Colombia became *Mas Familias en Acción*; Mexico's *Progresa* first became *Oportunidades* and then *Prospera; Chile Solidario* was renamed *Ingreso Etico Familiar.* In some sense the name change reflects the programs' strong civic capacity and political support: politicians in

© The Author(s) 2017
M. Morais de Sá e Silva, *Poverty Reduction, Education, and the Global Diffusion of Conditional Cash Transfers*, DOI 10.1007/978-3-319-53094-9_8

office want to reap the political dividends of running the program and therefore want constituents to relate program impacts to his/her own administration.

Hence, to some extent, similar arguments can be used to explain both part of CCTs' diffusion, as well as their long survival in various countries, especially where lack of funding has not been a reason for their early termination. Wherever funding was not an issue, programs were and have been able to survive for long years.

Now, the question is what will happen next to these programs. Do their results speak for themselves and will allow them to stay around for much longer? Or are there new factors that could possibly threaten their survival after this long wave—both in time and space—of their global diffusion?

On the bright side are two strong current trends that may help CCTs' continued existence: evidence-based policymaking and the use of behavioral insights in policy design. So first, the idea that policy decision and formulation should be informed by evidence has actually fueled a number of CCT evaluations and, in some cases, CCT experiments were actually created to inform program adoption in the first place. Besides, the more one measures CCT impacts, the more there will be a need to twist and tweak the program and continue it, so that a new assessment can be made. Also, as CCTs are such LEGO-like programs, there are endless possibilities in terms of program design for each country, province, or city. In other words, a CCT program could have its existence extended for numerous years on the basis of a trial-and-error evidence-based rationale.

Moreover, the strengthening of the "Nudge" approach to policymaking can well encompass and take CCTs to a next new level. Nudge researchers and followers have worked around the benefits of behavioral insights to policy, studying, among other things, how governments can induce citizens to "do the right thing" or at least to comply with an expected or desirable pattern of behavior. According to Thaler and Sunstein (2008), "it is legitimate for choice architects to try to influence people's behavior in order to make their lives longer, healthier, and better" (p. 5).

To some extent, the very idea of making cash transfers conditional upon the fulfillment of conditionalities could be considered as involving nudge, or shall we call it nudge with a premium? CCTs fit into the rationale of choice architecture, whereby the good or right individual choices can be induced or receive a nudge. In New York, Opportunity NYC was a—failed—attempt at the implementation of a program testing various sorts of nudges with a premium. Most of them did not have an impact and, even though the program was terminated for that same reason, a smaller and tweaked version of it is still being tested in the city and studied by MDRC.

So one possibility is that CCTs maintain—or even expand—their global reach by latching on to a new agenda: that of evidence-based policymaking linked to behavioral insights. In such a case, they may continue their spread not only to new countries, but also to provinces and cities, taking the shape of smaller trials. Funding could become increasingly available, coming not only from international organizations but also from national and foreign research foundations. As mentioned earlier in Chaps. 1 and 2, part of this trend is already happening, as demonstrated by more recent CCTs created in African countries as a part of experiments designed by foreign researchers.

However, if that new agenda becomes a safer ground vis-à-vis the poverty-reduction agenda, one of the direct consequences is that CCTs may lose sight of their equity and equality-oriented goals.They may keep diffusing but rather within a framework of experimentation and a quest for the perfect CCT design. Also, they may be transformed from cash transfers with attached conditions to nudges with a cash prize. In other words, if the heart of CCTs is currently the idea of a cash transfer for poverty reduction, their central idea may rather become the induction of—any—behavior through cash payments. In education for instance, this may mean the spread of experiments such as Opportunity NYC's Spark subprogram, where cash is used to induce student behavior toward more effort and better grades.

However, if research seems to offer a bright yet fuzzy future for CCTs, politics is rather dooming. The increasing number of conservative governments in Latin America and in other countries may reverse the pattern of decades of large-scale CCTs. First, various governments, such as the post-impeachment administration in Brazil, have tightened their budget belts and adopted austerity measures. Although CCTs have proven quite cost-effective, giving out cash may become contradictory with a restrictive fiscal policy. Brazil's *Bolsa Família*, for instance, benefits 14 million families and yet uses only 0.5% of the country's GDP and about 2.5% of the total government expenditure. Nonetheless, as mentioned in Chap. 6, the new administration has already taken measures to scrutinize the beneficiary database so as to exclude as many families in an irregular situation as possible.

In an era of political extremism, especially with the rise of open-and-proud conservatism, there is an elevated risk of backlash against CCTs, as the agenda they originated from no longer counts among dominant political support. The impeachment of DilmaRousseff in Brazil, the election of Donald Trump in the US, the victory of the No vote in Colombia may be signs that we are moving away from a long legitimated agenda of socially progressive regimes. What will that mean for the global poverty-reduction agenda and, consequently, for CCTs?

As discussed in Chap. 1, poverty reduction has not always been on the international and national agendas, as it only gained space and support with the evolution and changes in the development framework. Hence, at some point in history—precisely in the 1990s—development came to be equivalent not only to modernization and prosperity but also to less poor and unequal societies. This perspective was reinforced with the concept of human development and the adoption of the Millennium Development Goals.

However, if this status quo changes, CCTs lose the agenda upon which they were built and diffused. There would be no reason to transfer cash to the poor if they are no longer a source of governmental concern and attention, if they are simply to work hard and wait patiently for the hopeful trickling down effect of supposedly growing economies.

In the US, Republicans have traditionally defended the idea of "pulling yourself by your bootstraps." That basic idea may in so many ways clash with the fundamentals of CCTs. If the economy and society as a whole are to follow a rationale of the survival of the fittest, then poverty is seen as a natural result for those who do not work hard enough. Hence, there would be no reason why the state should intervene in order to combat poverty and include the poor in the education system, for instance.

All this occurs at a time when public opinion is formed through misinformation that easily navigates through Whatsapp messages and social media. Hence, civic support that proved to be strong around these programs for the past 10–20 years may rapidly erode. The whole idea of welfare dependence, which CCTs have often been accused of, may for once find fertile soil and flourish.

Here, the role of international organizations will again be very crucial. As discussed throughout this book, they have been important entrepreneurs for CCTs' global diffusion and have in many cases created the conditions for their adoption. At a first stage, there are reasons to believe that international organizations and donors will maintain their support for CCTs. However, once the governing bodies of these organizations start having their members replaced with representatives of new conservative governments, the pro-CCT policy and discourse may come to change, especially if the poverty reduction platform loses ground.

Although all of this may seem mere speculation, the analysis carried out in this book for the past 20 years of CCT existence and global diffusion leads one to the conclusion that such a pattern was only possible because there was a solid and dominating international agenda for poverty reduction. CCTs' flexibility also helped them travel and survive political change in national administrations, but an important part of their strength comes from a common ground where less poverty and more education are unquestionably seen as a social goal to be pursued by governments with the use of public money. If that chain of reasoning is broken or if that social contract is revoked, CCTs' global castle may prove to be actually sand castles.

REFERENCE

Thaler, R., & Sunstein, C. (2008). *Nudge: Improving decisions about health, wealth, and happiness*. New York: Penguin Books.

INDEX

© The Editor(s) (if applicable) and The Author(s) 2017
M. Morais de Sá e Silva, *Poverty Reduction, Education, and the Global Diffusion of Conditional Cash Transfers*, DOI 10.1007/978-3-319-53094-9